SWIMMING WILD

IN THE
LAKE DISTRICT

SWIMMING WILD

IN THE
LAKE DISTRICT

THE MOST BEAUTIFUL WILD SWIMMING
SPOTS IN THE LARGER LAKES

SUZANNA CRUICKSHANK

Vertebrate Publishing, Sheffield
www.v-publishing.co.uk

SWIMMING WILD IN THE LAKE DISTRICT

THE MOST BEAUTIFUL WILD SWIMMING SPOTS IN THE LARGER LAKES

First published in 2020 by Vertebrate Publishing. Reprinted in 2021.

VERTEBRATE PUBLISHING
Omega Court, 352 Cemetery Road, Sheffield S11 8FT, United Kingdom.
www.v-publishing.co.uk

A CIP catalogue record for this book is available from the British Library.

ISBN 978-1-912560-62-2 (Paperback)
ISBN 978-1-912560-75-2 (Ebook)

Front cover: High Crag across Buttermere.
Back cover: L–R: Buttermere © Suzanna Cruickshank; Coniston Water; Rosie Shark Dog;
Derwent Water © Ashia Cannon; Rydal Water; Loweswater Gold © Andrew Locking;
Waking up, Windermere style!; The original lady of the lake, Jude Gale, at Derwent Water © Stuart Holmes.

Photography by Stewart Smith except where otherwise credited.

Maps produced by Don Williams of Bute Cartographics.
Contains Ordnance Survey data © Crown copyright and database right 2020.

Design by Jane Beagley, production by Cameron Bonser, Vertebrate Publishing.

Printed and bound in China by Latitude Press.

Vertebrate Publishing is committed to printing on paper from sustainable sources.

Opposite High Peel Near, Coniston Water

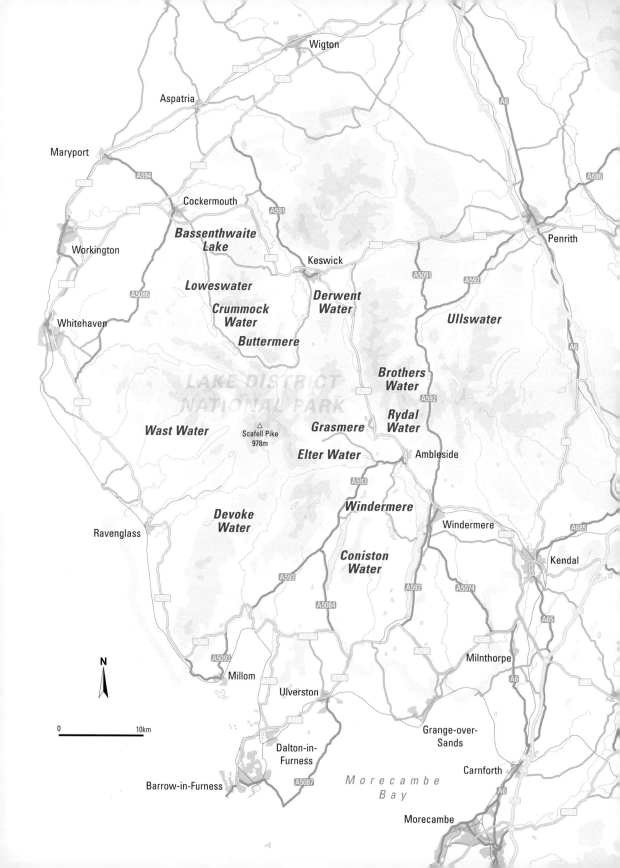

Opposite Otterbield Bay, Derwent Water **Below** Above and below in Buttermere © Suzanna Cruickshank

Introduction

'Is it safe?' – my dad on the subject of any swim; any lake. His idea of safe was tied with that of permission and common knowledge. He never said this about hills. There was always a guidebook to read and a map to follow for hills.

My dad was in the terminal stages of prostate cancer when the outline for this guidebook was conceived. As he became less able to climb hills, we took shorter, easier walks. I started to swim more. He would nervously watch from the water's edge, always more confident of my ability to drown than my ability to swim.

Like many a good idea, the idea to write this guidebook was dreamt up in a pub. I'd just been for a hair-raising and ill-advised swim near a fast-flowing weir on a windy November afternoon. It was the most terrified I had ever been in the water, and indeed have been since. In the pub afterwards, Dad – clearly troubled by the particular shade of white my face was when I returned to shore – ruminated, 'There should be a book – one that tells you where it's safe to get in'. And there wasn't, not a dedicated Lake District book anyway.

So the idea was born. Researching material for this book kept me sane as the demands of caring grew. The idea it would ever reach publication was fanciful, and after my dad passed away I threw myself into building my fledgling swim business and all the qualifications that entailed. I'm proud that my fanciful idea has become a reality.

In the adventurous spirit of wild swimming, this is not an exhaustive guide to every single location around every single lake. You can swim anywhere in the Lake District where you are able to access the water without trespassing. Ordnance Survey maps are invaluable for planning swim adventures. But the mere existence of access does not mean you should swim. Whether it is 'safe' depends on you, the swimmer, and conditions on the day. Remember, if an easily accessed section of lakeshore looks undesirable, a gem might be just round the corner.

I hope you will use this guidebook to explore the highlights of each lake and find your own favourite. Happy swimming!

Wild swimming in the Lake District

Swimmers have migrated from natural waters to the confines of indoor lanes, and back again, for over 200 years. The fashion for 'taking the waters' for one's wellbeing can be traced back to the seventeenth century when seaside dips were promoted as a cure for many ills, and the medicinal value of spring-fed spa bathing became popular. This trend virtually passed Cumbria by with only local populations travelling to Cumbrian seaside resorts. Even on the sunniest August day it must have been a tough sell to pass off the grey coastal waters as highly beneficial for health. Tourists were not flocking to the Lake District for the lakes in the nineteenth century, but for the hills. Contemplation of the mountain landscape was very much in vogue and, guidebook in hand, visitors would follow set itineraries across the Lake District to particular viewpoints.

Undoubtedly people did swim in the lakes, or at least bathe, but little has been recorded. The British Long Distance Swimming Association was formed in 1956 and has had strong links to the Lake District since its inception. It's an unequivocally outdoor swimming association. I'm grateful to their secretary, Vince, who was able to give me some interesting historical information including the earliest recorded swim in Windermere when Joseph Foster swam the entire length of the lake in 1911. Countless other records followed with efforts focused on Bassenthwaite Lake, Coniston Water, Derwent Water, Ullswater and Windermere.

I spoke to friends who grew up in Cumbria to find out about their swimming experiences as children. Schoolchildren in Keswick, Ambleside and Coniston during the 1970s and 1980s would have learned in a swimming pool, although

1 Autumnal Grasmere **2** Throwing shapes © Suzanna Cruickshank
3 Wast Water **4** Getting ready for a swim © Anita Nicholson **5** Wild Crummock Water © Carmen Norman

lessons were also held in lakes in warmer months. For their parents' generation, lessons were held in a lake. With no such things as wetsuits, they swam as quickly as they possibly could between the jetties until they were allowed to get out again.

On Windermere, a swimming club was situated at Millerground and Rayrigg Meadow. The changing huts still stand there now. Windermere Bathing Pool was where countless local children learned to swim in pre- and post-World War II years. Once the indoor pool opened in nearby Troutbeck Bridge during the post-war boom, lake swimming popularity waned and was actively discouraged as swimmers flocked to the modern facilities. This matched the trend for the rest of the country with nearly 200 public pools being built between 1960 and 1970. Today, Keswick Leisure Pool and Askham Outdoor Swimming Pools

are the only public pools within the Lake District National Park boundary. The swimming pool at Troutbeck Bridge fell into disrepair in the 1990s; it is now a membership-based health club.

When my interest in taking my short dips further was piqued, I went in search of information. The existing wild swimming guidebooks were undoubtedly well researched but the handful of Lake District locations they contained were ones I already knew. Internet searches turned up vague locations and repetitive descriptions. Joining a club seemed way above my skill set with training drills and the ominous 'tri' in many club titles. So I set out to do it myself.

Ever since Thomas West published *A Guide to the Lakes* in 1778, countless others have published their take on the Lake District and what makes it so special. Now it's my turn.

Getting started in open water

My love of the outdoors stems from many hours spent walking in the hills, enjoying the sheer simplicity of self-propelled progress over interesting terrain. Skills obtained in this area are transferable – interpreting a map or weather forecast, for example. Going for a walk is as easy as putting one foot in front of the other. Making the transition from fully clothed on a lakeshore to full submersion is quite different. Dipping your toes into wild water is a step into the unknown. It forces you to leave the reliable gravitational pull of dry land and put your faith into something intangible.

It's at this stage that for the first-time wild swimmer I recommend hiring the services of a reputable guide. Someone who has swum in those waters many times, who maybe has their own guiding business. They might have even written a guidebook telling you all about swimming in the Lake District! But scan any wild swimming website or forum and you'll see that variations of the question 'how do I start wild swimming' are popular. A frequent reply is 'go with a friend' and 'just get in'. So, like most people, I didn't hire a guide. I just got in.

My first foray into open water was in Bassenthwaite Lake. I don't think I had ever heard the term wild swimming before, I was simply going for a swim outside. I dipped a tentative toe in the water and then spent several minutes psyching myself up to get fully submerged. I swam in frantic circles for what felt like an age, but was probably no more than a few minutes, before I hurried out again.

For the next few years that was the sum total of my wild swimming experiences. Quick hesitant dips in the heat of summer, always tinged with a slight sense of 'there must be more to this'. Then, in the same way that my friends Liam and Kath had handed me a guidebook to expand my horizons beyond the familiar paths of Whinlatter Forest, my friend Jude took me for a proper swim in Derwent Water and changed the way I looked at water forever.

Like a writer sitting down to tackle the beginning, middle and end of their story, planning a swim should feature a before, during and after.

Opposite Max and Grace take flight at Ashness Jetty, Derwent Water

Before

» **Preparation starts at home**, by checking the weather and ground conditions and packing your bag.

» **Consider the extra energy swimming in cold water will require**; don't forget to fuel your body appropriately for the activity.

» **Don't underestimate how cold you might feel after leaving the water.** Pack warm clothes to wear after your swim, and arrive warm. Some of my most uncomfortable swims were the ones where I was cold before I entered the water and subsequently took hours to warm up.

» **Always let someone know where you are going** and try not to swim alone. There are lots of social swim groups across the country, far more than when I first started. Find people on social media or contact the Outdoor Swimming Society to find a local group. If you really can't find anyone to get in the water with you, take someone to watch. I bought my dad a throw line – a twenty-metre length of floating rope that can be used as a rescue aid by a supporter on the shore. He found this reassuring knowing that he could confidently throw the line should I need it, and not risk getting into the water himself.

» **Don't drink and drown.** As well as lowering your perception of risk, having alcohol in your system impairs your body's ability to regulate its temperature. Ditto drugs.

» **Identify your entry and exit points.** Can you get out as easily as you can get in? If the lake bed shelves suddenly you could find yourself in deep water before you are ready for it.

» **Get in slowly, don't jump.** Leaping in might make a great Instagram photo, but if you are unacclimatised or unaccustomed to cold water, this is the quickest way to suffer cold water shock, which can be fatal. Get in slowly and splash yourself with water. Control your breathing and avoid gulping air as you fully submerge. Never jump in without first checking the depth, even in a location you are familiar with or have jumped in before. Lake levels fluctuate significantly after rain.

» **Protect your belongings** from the elements while you swim. Worried some naughty rascals might run off with your clothes? Or a nosy labrador will steal your sandwiches? In busier places I use a camouflage dry bag to hide things in the undergrowth or I pop my clothes in an inflatable swim bag and take them with me. I've never had my clothes stolen, or my mobile phone and car keys for that matter, but someone did walk off with my fire pit while I was in the River Derwent. Try fitting that in a swim bag!

» **Biosecurity** is a vital issue in the Lake District. Make sure you read the advice on page xxv before you get started.

I often spend longer researching a swim than actually doing it. This is especially true in winter when there are more risks to weigh up. Research is part of the fun for me, scouring the map for tiny hidden bays and using apps to track the trajectory of the sun for that perfect sunrise or sunset location through the seasons.

Below Swimmers at Peel Wyke, Bassenthwaite Lake © Anita Nicholson

During

» **Are there other users on the lake?** I try to avoid swimming where I might come across boat traffic, but if it's unavoidable make yourself as noticeable as possible. Wear a brightly coloured cap, use a tow float and attach a whistle. Consider taking a friend in a kayak or on a paddleboard.

» **Know your limits**. Tempting as it is, especially on a warm day, don't stay in too long or overestimate your ability. It's better to leave a lake feeling like you could have stayed in longer, than not leaving the lake at all. Similarly, don't be tempted to swim out into the middle of a lake on your first swim. It's always further than you think. Build your confidence by swimming parallel to the shore.

» **How far are you planning to swim?** It's easier to stay in longer than you intended if you are with a mixed ability group. Be cautious of overt and subliminal peer pressure and don't feel you should swim outside your comfort zone to keep up appearances. If you are used to swimming a certain distance in a pool you may find this significantly reduced in open water due to water temperature and weather conditions. I find wearing a simple stopwatch helpful and track my swim time rather than distance.

» **Weeds** are a common fear amongst swimmers but getting tangled beyond release is unlikely. If you swim into weeds, let your legs drift and float over them, either sculling gently with your hands or using breaststroke arms.

» **Currents** are not usually an issue in lakes. In large bodies of water the flow is slow. You are more likely to be pushed off course by wind than a lake current. Be careful where rivers flow into a lake; be aware of the potential for them to push you away from the shore. Islands and narrow channels can speed up the flow of water and you should avoid swimming near weirs. In a lake setting currents should be a general awareness rather than a grave danger.

1 Post-swim drink © James Kirby   **2** Swimming socks and shoes © Carmen Norman
3 Swimming bag © Carmen Norman

After

» **Don't hang around** once you get out, especially if it is windy. Your body cools down more quickly when wet and exposed to cold air, and hypothermia is a very real risk even in summer.

» **Wrap up well** even on a mild day – you continue to cool down for around thirty minutes after leaving the water. Put on all your warm clothes even if you feel fine initially.

» **Remember to Check, Clean and Dry** (see page xxv).

» **Have a hot drink** and something to eat. The feel-good factor in consuming something warm and tasty also serves a scientific purpose. Our bodies generate heat by metabolising food. If that's not an excuse to eat a pie then I don't know what is.

This before, during and after advice is a potted version of what I teach on beginner open-water sessions in my day job as a swimming guide. It's mostly common sense but should not be considered the final word in how to swim safely outdoors. That part is up to you, the swimmer. Further resources are available from the Royal Life Saving Society, the Royal National Lifeboat Institution, and the Outdoor Swimming Society. In particular, the OSS has a wealth of informative articles on its website written for and by wild swimmers.

» *www.rlss.org.uk*
» *www.rnli.org*
» *www.outdoorswimmingsociety.com*

Wild swimming is one of the most liberating things you can do. Plan carefully then get out there and enjoy the lakes!

1

SAFETY

In the event of an emergency in the Lake District dial **999** or **112** and ask for the **Police**, then **Mountain Rescue**. (This advice will vary in other parts of the UK depending on what services are available in that location.)

Where possible give a six-figure grid reference of your location and that of the casualty. In the UK you can also contact the emergency services by SMS text – useful if you have low battery or intermittent signal. You need to register your phone first by texting 'register' to 999 and then following the instructions in the reply. Do it now – it could save yours or someone else's life.

www.emergencysms.net

Equipment

One of the most basic joys of swimming is that it requires virtually no specialist equipment at all.* At the very least you need a swimming costume or trunks. Some would argue you need nothing at all.

Swimming is a great leveller; you need very little to get started and most of it is left behind as you swim.

Outdoor swimming can be as basic or as technical as you like. Wetsuits are often pooh-poohed by purists as 'cheating' – they say that the only way to swim outside is in your trunks or not at all. It's true that many competitions and challenges set a 'no wetsuit' rule, but I say whatever gets you in the water. Wear what you feel comfortable in, whether that is a thermal wetsuit and balaclava, or a bikini. Indeed, both appear in this guidebook!

I try not to take much notice of reviews or opinions lauding a particular brand or product as 'the best'. The thing that is the best is the one that works best for you. I have made an exception in recommending a particular brand of socks and gloves as I have tried many and these are the best … the best for me!

Suzanna's kit list
» **Swimsuit/trunks**
» **Wetsuit (optional)**
» **Goggles**
» **Swimming cap**
» **Thermal accessories if it's cold (gloves and socks)**
» **Tow float/dry bag**
» **Changing robe/sports towel**
» **Whistle**
» **Earplugs**

Optional extras
» **Phone case/waterproof camera**
» **Waterproof roll-top bag**
» **Swimming shoes**

* A quick internet search for open-water swimming will discount this statement immediately. There are socks, gloves, thermal vests, thermal caps, tow floats, goggles, robes, bags and changing mats. What is the best wetsuit for a beginner? What thickness of socks are best for swimming in winter? How do you stop your goggles steaming up? What is the best swimming cap for long hair? Like most ostensibly simple sports or pastimes, once you dig a little deeper it's clear that outdoor swimmers like a nice shiny bit of a kit as much as the next runner, cyclist or fell walker.

Wetsuits and swimsuits

Mostly, I swim in a swimsuit. It's not for everyone, and it can take time to acclimatise. Depending on the conditions I might also wear a thin neoprene vest, and add a pair of thermal gloves and socks when it is truly baltic.

An entry-level wetsuit costs around £80 and you can pay well over £500 for an elite suit. Luckily, there is plenty of choice in the middle ground of this range and it pays to speak to the experts before you buy. Swim the Lakes in Ambleside run events where you can try on wetsuits; they also offer an excellent fitting service in the shop, and a nice cup of tea. Bespoke wetsuits come with rave reviews and are not that much more expensive than a decent off-the-peg wetsuit. Expect to pay upwards of £300 for a made-to-measure wetsuit.

My first wetsuit was a cheap surfing wetsuit. I hated it with a passion and it was soon consigned to the bin. It was a couple of years before I went for a fitting and bought a proper swimming wetsuit. While perfectly acceptable for swimming in, surf and general water sports wetsuits are usually thicker and less flexible. They have not been designed with swimming or full submersion in mind. The more you swim in them the more you will become aware of their limitations. Swimming wetsuits have a smooth finish for gliding through the water and stretchy panels for arm rotation and easy removal. For extra warmth you can wear a rash vest or neoprene vest underneath, or there are some excellent thermal wetsuits available if you really feel the cold.

When you go for a fitting it's important to tell the fitter what kind of swimming you do and your predominant stroke. Wetsuits are available with lower buoyancy and better leg flex for breaststroke swimmers, as well as super buoyancy to lift trailing legs and stretchy shoulders to aid front crawl.

Goggles

Even if you don't intend swimming with your face in the water, it's a good idea to have some goggles so you can at least dip your head in to see what you are swimming over. There can be hidden hazards such as boulders, logs, debris or trailing weeds; it's sensible to stay aware of your surroundings as you swim.

Style comes down to personal preference. Traditional socket goggles are cheap and easily replaced. Mask-style goggles are more expensive, but they give a greater field of vision often preferred by open-water swimmers. The wider face coverage also provides more protection against the dreaded ice cream headache.

Swimming cap

A swimming cap is a personal choice if you are just dipping in and out. A brightly coloured swimming cap is advisable when swimming in lakes where there are boats. As well as keeping your hair dry and your head warm it makes you visible to other lake users. The boathands on the Keswick Launch prefer bright neon colours. They are less keen on white, silver or blue as these colours become difficult to pick out on a sunny day. If you submerge your head while swimming, protect your ears from cold and infection with earplugs. Trapped water is unpleasant and can lead to infections requiring antibiotics. This is commonly known as *swimmer's ear*. It shouldn't be confused with *surfer's ear* which is abnormal bone growth caused by repeated exposure to cold water. This can only be fixed with surgery.

1 Leaving the water © James Kirby   **2** The only swimming cap to be seen in © James Kirby

Gloves and socks

Many swimmers I have spoken to don't like the sensation of wearing gloves in the water, or find they hamper their stroke. Bare hands become a useful indicator for when it's time to leave the water. Front crawlers' gloves need to be snug to prevent them billowing and filling with water on each downwards stroke, using either a wrist strap to tighten them or worn tucked into the sleeves of a wetsuit. I'm predominately a breaststroke swimmer so fit is less of an issue and gloves often act as a hand paddle aiding each stroke. I developed Raynaud's disease a couple of years ago and tried all the gloves on the market, settling on C-Skins as the gold standard, for me anyway!

When it comes to socks, C-Skins Legends are, well, the stuff of legend. With a thick lining and reinforced sole they are my first choice for cool conditions. I have broken ice on high tarns wearing them. The rest of me came out screaming but my toes were toasty. Usually though I love the freedom of swimming barefoot and only really wear thermal socks when it's bone-crushingly cold, or for work when I might be more static in the water.

Look out for socks with a reinforced sole to extend their lifespan. They also help if, like me, you are squeamish about touching weeds or mud.

Swimming shoes

Many swimmers favour swimming shoes to help negotiate the rocky edges of lakes and waters. Litter can also be an issue in many popular spots. Look for moulded plastic or jelly shoes which have no fabric and dry easily, thus avoiding the transfer of invasive species between lakes.

Tow floats and dry bags

As well as a swimming cap, a tow float aids your visibility in the water. A large range of floats are available, from a straightforward tow float to different sizes of inflatable, submersible dry bags. Puffin Swim have developed the first eco-friendly tow float that can be composted at the end of its life. Tow floats and inflatable dry bags also give you a 'pool edge' to hold on to when you're out in a lake, allowing you to rest and catch your breath when you can't put your feet down. They float behind you creating minimal drag as you swim and the dry bags are big enough to carry clothes and a towel, and even your packed lunch. Using these bags, I have swum across lakes and down rivers, freed from the restriction of having to return to where I left my clothes. Remember, a tow float is not a substitute for ability. It is only as safe as the swimmer it is attached to.

Changing robes and towels

With a lack of formal changing facilities, wild swimmers become adept at ducking behind trees to change as quickly as possible before anyone catches a glimpse of a bare bum cheek. Surf ponchos, essentially two giant beach towels stitched together, effortlessly maintain your dignity while you change at the side of a lake or by the boot of your car and are less likely to blow away than a normal towel.

The ubiquitous outerwear of choice amongst outdoor swimmers is the waterproof insulated sports cloak. Such is their popularity that the leading brand name is used interchangeably to describe all kinds of après-swim wear from towelling ponchos to other brands of sports cloaks and coats. Voluminous and warm, they are a generous fit for use as your own personal changing tent, and large enough to wear over your clothes and coat.

They are undoubtedly useful for rewarming after a swim and sheltering from the elements. Me? I am still getting used to mine. It's a tad unwieldy and my overriding preference is to warm up on the move and carry everything I need in my backpack.

Extras

Apart from the items I have bought specially for use in open-water swimming, most of the other things you will find in my bag are things I own and use for other activities. My rucksack itself, base layers, thermals and a down jacket. Roll-top waterproof bags are handy for carrying wet kit or keeping dry things dry. As with many outdoor activities where you can go from cold to hot and back again in a short space of time, layering is key and wearing several thin layers serves me better than a single thick layer. I don't need an excuse to pull on thermal leggings and I relish wearing a vest. Suffering from Raynaud's disease has led me to conduct extensive glove research and spend a small fortune in Keswick-based Needle Sports – where better to find warm gloves that allow dexterity in cold conditions than a dedicated climbing shop?

Over the years, I have come to realise that swimming is usually the easy bit. What you do before and after plays a big part in your success and enjoyment. Your ability to get warm after a swim is far more important than what brand of goggles you buy. If in doubt, throw an extra layer, hat and a pair of gloves in your bag. It's better to have them and not need them than find yourself or someone else in desperate need and lacking.

1 Mask-style goggles © Carmen Norman   **2** Swimming bag © James Kirby
3 Be bright and visible © James Kirby   **4** Gloves for colder conditions © Carmen Norman
5 Towelling robe © Carmen Norman   **6** The author's favourite swimming shoes © James Kirby

Geology & ecology – or 'why are the lakes different colours?'

For such a relatively small area, the Lake District is a complex and varied beast. The region's underlying geology is made up of igneous, metamorphic and sedimentary rocks, heavily eroded by glacial action to give us the distinctive landscape we see today. Each lake and its parent valley radiate imperfectly from the central massif with all but the eastern areas linking to the central massif. How the landforms of the Lake District were created might not be of immediate interest to swimmers, but they have everything to do with the water you swim in. The subject is a tricky one to unpick. I didn't study geography past the age of thirteen at school; who knows if it would have helped me with this chapter! There are some very informative books on the subject listed on page 164 if you wish to delve deeper.

While all the lakes have very obvious similarities, their individual characters are defined by their immediate environment. The water appears to be a different colour from lake to lake and the clarity is hugely varied. I can't remember the exact moment of awe when I first swam in Buttermere, but I know I have felt it on every swim since. Dunking my head under the water invokes unspeakable joy and a stream of bubbles from my exclamations at the pristine water. Each body of water has a unique smell and taste. Some lakes I don't mind if I end up drinking them, in others my mouth stays clamped shut. The clues are in the landscape, both geological and man-made. Grab a handful of rock in Buttermere or Ullswater and you will find it smooth and hard. It won't crumble easily if crushed together or create sediment through friction. These are valleys of

1 Underwater in Derwent Water © Suzanna Cruickshank   **2** Crummock Water shoreline
3 Low sedimentation in Crummock Water © Stuart Holmes

compellingly raw scenery with prominent peaks and fierce crags. The rock is older and harder, offering the most resistance against glacial processes. You will find the deepest lakes here. Lakes formed in areas of younger sedimentary rock are the result of greater denudation, creating softer, less dramatic scenery and gentler depths.

Broadly speaking, the hard and soft rock allows us to place the lakes into two groups, indicating the amount of biological activity they sustain – oligotrophic lakes and mesotrophic lakes. The combined geological and ecological influences are key contributors to the trophic status of a body of water. Solid igneous and granite bedrock provides the perfect conditions for an oligotrophic lake, one that is very low in nutrients with alkaline pH, making it inhospitable to extensive plant life. Softer sedimentary areas are home to mesotrophic lakes which have moderate levels of plant and algae growth. These lakes are susceptible to eutrophication. Eutrophication of a lake

is aided by human activity, both farming and domestic. Excess levels of phosphates and nitrates entering lakes encourage plant growth and algae bloom which can lead to silt building up and shallower depths. Eutrophic lakes also tend to be milder in temperature. They are usually shallower with a thicker layer of silt on the bottom, and further away from the water source, all factors in water temperature.

Wast Water owes its impeccably clear water not just to the source element and surrounding bedrock, but to the low number of people living in the lake catchment. Their domestic activities have minimal impact on the lake and farming is carefully managed – ensuring minimal agricultural input affects the protected status of Wast Water. The lake's low temperature and nutrient-poor water sustains very little life. While Wast Water is inhospitable to most species, it allows the nationally rare Arctic char to flourish in its chilly depths.

Bassenthwaite Lake, on the other hand, is described as a mesotrophic lake in its Site of Special Scientific Interest (SSSI) designation,

but is prone to eutrophication if left unchecked. The lake was the subject of a recent lake restoration case study and is in an improving state. The large and varied catchment of Bassenthwaite carries sediment and excess phosphates into the lake. Increased sediment leads to a soft silty coating on the bottom of the lake. It creates a thermal layer, provides a basis for plants to grow, or simply for more sediment to settle and diminish the depth of the water. These factors increase algae activity that can harm the health of the lake. Steps have been taken to protect the lake, including tree planting to reduce erosion and improved sewerage systems in the catchment area to reduce phosphates.

Nutrient-rich lakes attract waterfowl with their abundant plant life, algae and other organisms for birds to feed on. Where there are plenty of ducks and geese, you can expect to find waterborne parasites looking for their next victim. Swimmer's itch, or cercarial dermatitis, is the scourge of swimmers. A quick dip, particularly in a swimsuit, can leave you riddled with bites. You can reduce the risk when swimming in mesotrophic lakes by wearing a wetsuit or rash vest, not swimming in areas with lots of wildfowl, avoiding hot days when activity will be high, or choosing another lake entirely. The inhospitable waters of oligotrophic lakes don't attract much wildlife or waterfowl. You will rarely, if ever, hear a swimmer complain of 'swimmer's itch' in oligotrophic lakes such as Wast Water or Buttermere.

Another feature of warm weather is the appearance of blue-green algae blooms. Most lakes have algae in them and they are an important part of the aquatic cycle. When the weather is warm and still, blooms occur on the surface and these can be toxic, particularly to dogs. They are easy to spot and can look like someone has poured paint in the lake. Warnings about blue-green algae often involve a blanket warning for an entire lake, but you should always carry out your own inspection. Areas of a lake with a steady supply of fresh water may not be affected. You can read more on blue-green algae in Loweswater on page 157.

Several lakes have an SSSI designation. Trying to find a definitive yes or no regarding swimming in an SSSI lake is often as clouded as the water. Natural England's stance is that recreational or other activities likely to damage water quality, vegetation, flora and fauna are not permitted. It is vital that swimmers do their research and approach SSSIs in a conscientious manner. This might mean choosing a different location, or even a different time of year.

Knowing a little about the geology will help you understand what you are swimming in and the ecology of that water. It can even help you make a decision on where to swim. Next time you are starfishing in the middle of a lake, look up. The clues to the water you are floating in are right there in the hills above you.

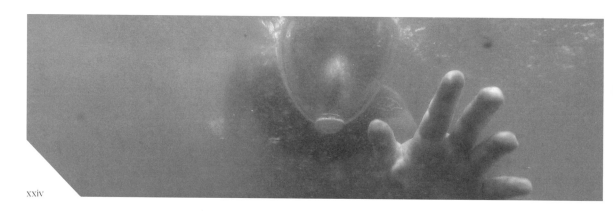

Biosecurity

The Lake District has an alien invasion. Non-native freshwater plants and animals are established in some of our lakes, rivers and tarns and are rapidly outcompeting native species. The danger of these invasive species is their tenacity. If removed from a body of water, they can survive for days or weeks in damp conditions, ready to take hold as soon as they reach water again.

Plants such as New Zealand pygmyweed (*Crassula helmsii*) are choking parts of Derwent Water despite efforts to remove it at regular intervals. It was first recorded in the lake in the 1990s and by 2003 it had displaced nine native species. The plant first came to the UK as a decorative garden plant and for use in aquariums. It's thought the initial transfer to the wild may have been someone unthinkingly emptying an aquarium into a river or lake, or it could have hitched a ride on a bird from a garden pond. The plant is now banned from sale in the UK.

New Zealand pygmyweed is only one of the offenders. Himalayan balsam, American skunk-cabbage, and non-native fish including ruffe and roach all have a detrimental effect on our lakes.

It's vital that swimmers are diligent in their post-swim routines. Our swimwear and associated accoutrements have many ways for invasive plant fragments and organisms to hitch a ride – goggle straps, waist belts, camera straps and so on. Swim shoes are a common culprit as plants easily become tangled in laces or straps. Alongside other lake users, biosecurity is a key responsibility of outdoor swimmers. The easy-to-remember three-point rule promoted by conservation agencies is Check, Clean and Dry.

Check – on leaving the water, check yourself and your equipment for hangers-on. This includes checking hair, footwear and tow floats.

Clean – remove any organic matter in-situ to avoid transferring it to another location. Even better, remove all your equipment and take it home to clean. Washing kit in-situ stops the spread to other locations but it means that plants are washed back into the water and will be able to re-establish themselves. A gold star solution is to take your swim kit home to check and rinse, away from a watercourse. Leaving plants and organisms to dry out and die is a small positive step towards recovery.

Dry – invasive species can survive in damp conditions, so it's best to dry your kit no matter how thoroughly you have washed and checked it.

As well as Check, Clean and Dry, conscientious swimmers can avoid cross-contamination between lakes by carrying two sets of swimwear or by careful planning of their route. On multi-swim routes, start at the top of the catchment area and move downstream; for example from Grasmere to Rydal Water then Windermere, or Buttermere into Crummock Water.

Information is often displayed in car parks and near water egress points.
 » *www.nonnativespecies.org/checkcleandry*
 » *http://cfinns.scrt.co.uk*
 » *www.scrt.co.uk*
 » *www.westcumbriariverstrust.org*

Opposite Churned-up Bassenthwaite Lake © Suzanna Cruickshank

BASSEN-THWAITE LAKE

Opposite Scarness Bay with Dodd behind   **Overleaf** The Calvert Trust buildings from Bassenthwaite Lake

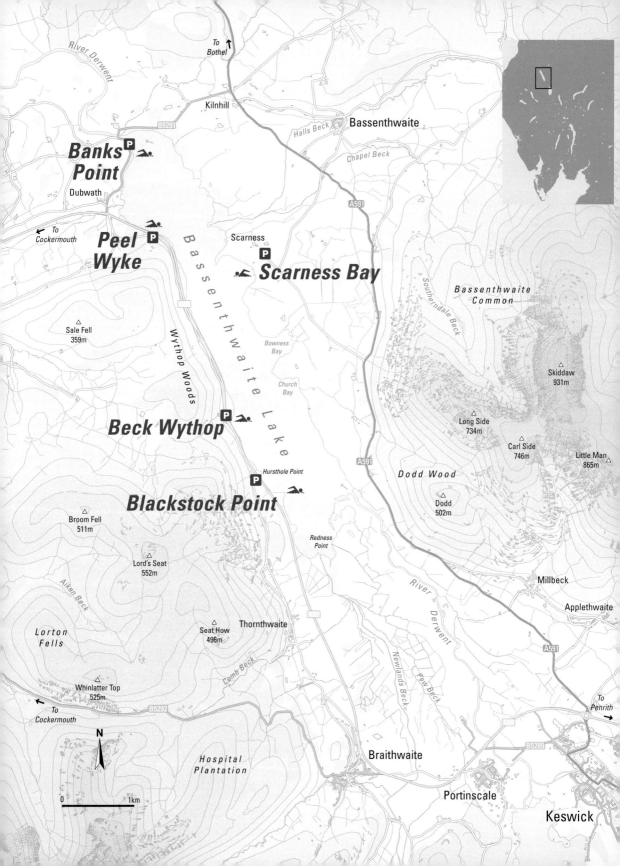

Introduction

'If it looks like a mountain and feels like a mountain, then it is a mountain.'
SIMON INGRAM, *BETWEEN THE SUNSET AND THE SEA.*

Bassenthwaite Lake, as many a pub quiz pedant will tell you, is the only 'real' lake in the Lake District. It is a lake in name while the rest are called 'meres' or 'waters', rendering pronouncements of 'Loweswater Lake' or 'Lake Windermere' incorrect. According to the Collins English Dictionary a lake is 'an expanse of water entirely surrounded by land and unconnected to the sea except by rivers or streams'. Fortunately, in this guide Bassenthwaite is first so I can avoid further tautological tangles and get this out of the way early. If it looks like a lake and feels like a lake … then go ahead and call it a lake. I won't correct you.

With the A66 trunk road on one side and mostly private land on the other, the lakeshore is less frequented than most. You will see dog walkers, fishermen and birdwatchers, but not the hordes of walkers found around Derwent Water, where you can easily say hello to a hundred people on a sunny Saturday. Bassenthwaite is the most northerly lake. It has no valley head and lies in a corridor of fells. Skiddaw is a benign presence above the lake, reclining genially along the eastern shore. One of Skiddaw's small satellites, Dodd, dominates the view and looks larger than its 502 metres. The airy ridge of Ullock Pike turns a vivid purple when the heather blooms. In the middle of the lake a wider view opens up encompassing the Helvellyn range, Cat Bells and Whinlatter Forest.

The water supplying Bassenthwaite Lake comes from as far away as Borrowdale, Thirlmere and all the way along the A66 to Troutbeck in the east. This is the largest catchment area of any of the lakes, covering some 139 square miles. Like Wast Water, Bassenthwaite is a 'coastal' lake, just ten miles to the Solway Firth as the crow flies. The surface is often dappled with a breeze and within the space of a few minutes tiny wavelets can be whipped up into big, face-slapping waves. Flat calm days are rare on Bassenthwaite.

Bassenthwaite Sailing Club enjoy the sole privilege of sailing on the lake, and there is no public right of navigation. Permits are needed to launch a boat and motorised boats are not allowed. Bowness Bay, on the eastern shore, and the head of the lake beyond Blackstock Point are protected breeding and nesting sites and closed to all. Of all the swimmable lakes in the Lake District, Bassenthwaite Lake is the longest body of water that is free from motor boats. This, coupled with the sheer ease of access, makes Bassenthwaite Lake one of my top picks.

Blackstock Point

The grassy peninsula is shaded from the road by noble oak trees and has a wide stony beach around the perimeter. It is a grand spot to park up and swim – from car to the water's edge in two minutes flat.

The entire lake is a designated National Nature Reserve. The head of the lake beyond Blackstock Point is a no-boating zone. You should also avoid swimming there so nesting or wintering birds are not disturbed.

As you might expect, being so close to the reed beds you are likely to see plenty of birdlife here – my favourites are mostly the ones I don't need a book to identify: cormorants, herons, goosander and great rafts of geese. You can also see (so I'm told) pochard, wigeon, goldeneye, tufted duck, great crested grebe, little grebe and red-breasted merganser. The star of the show is the osprey – it is a real treat to see their languorous circling over the lake. After a nest platform was built in Wythop Woods, a pair of ospreys nested there in 2001, becoming the first wild osprey to breed in the Lake District for over 150 years. Ospreys have nested in Wythop Woods and Dodd Wood ever since.

Blackstock Point is served by a convenient lay-by on the A66 (note that this lay-by can only be accessed when travelling north-west to south-east, i.e. from Cockermouth towards Keswick).

Opposite Hursthole Point **Below** Cat Bells across the lake from Scarness Bay

Beck Wythop

Another handy lay-by on the A66 (note that this lay-by can only be accessed when travelling north-west to south-east, i.e. from Cockermouth towards Keswick). There are steps down from the road to a gate and then a faint path bears to the right through thick undergrowth and elder trees. There is not much in the way of a beach but there are several small stony bays from which to launch yourself into the water. The lake bed is rough underfoot but the water deepens quickly, unlike other places around the lake.

Directly across the water is the beautiful little church of St Bega's. It is around 900 metres to the opposite shore – great for more experienced swimmers looking to stretch out on a longer swim.

Peel Wyke

A concrete slipway beneath a busy road bridge is a fairly incongruous location for wild swimming, however Peel Wyke is actually a rather fine place for a swim. It is favoured by many local swimmers for its convenience. I like to swim here all year round, appreciating the quiet when other locations are overrun in summer, and the shelter from the elements in winter. Stepping off the edge of the slipway into shallow water, the sediment immediately swells and swirls around your feet, while overhead cars rush by on the A66. The turbid water soon calms as you wade deeper; the road noise fades, and a lovely view opens up to your right. A wide fan of shallow water around the slipway makes this location suitable for swimmers who prefer to remain within their depth.

After your swim make time to climb Castle How. Follow the faint path behind the hut in the car park to the summit; it is a five-minute walk. The top has been artificially flattened – dating back to its past use as an Iron Age hillfort. Trees and bilberry bushes have grown to form a pretty fairy glen, perfect for a picnic. The car park is right by the water and is accessed from a slip road off the A66 (follow signs for the Pheasant Inn) – the car park is east of the pub, near the junction with the A66.

Banks Point

This western corner of the lake is where the water flows out to the River Derwent. You are unlikely to be troubled by sailing club activity in this area of the lake but be aware of kayakers and paddleboarders leaving the lake and heading down the river. There are two gravel lay-bys for parking on the B5291 south of Ouse Bridge with handy information boards telling you about the rich variety of bird activity on the lake. Don't forget your binoculars! A gently inclined gravel path leads off the car park and meets stone steps which take you down to the shore. The lake is shallow around this section of shore but there is a noticeable current from the River Derwent, especially after rain. Weak swimmers, paddlers and children should be supervised.

Scarness Bay

Tucked away along a wooded path lies Scarness Bay, our sole eastern shore location. It is a mile off the main road and right next to a holiday lodge park, yet it retains the air of a well-kept local secret, with the water hidden until the very last minute.

There is a small lay-by for several cars and a signpost next to the entrance of the holiday lodge park directs you through the wood to where the water laps the end of the path (250 metres). Adjacent to the path is an open field and wildflower meadow with a further path to a bench where non-swimmers can take in the view.

In spring, the way to the water is lined with fragrant wild garlic that I harvest by the handful on my way home. The lake bed is soft underfoot with a few stray boulders as the water gently deepens.

Technical information

MAXIMUM DEPTH **19 metres**   AVERAGE DEPTH **5.3 metres**   LENGTH **3.89 miles**   MAXIMUM WIDTH **0.68 miles**
PRIMARY INFLOWS **River Derwent, Newlands Beck, Chapel Beck**   OUTFLOW **River Derwent at Ouse Bridge**

Getting there
The X4 and X5 buses that run between Penrith, Keswick, Cockermouth and Workington serve both sides of the lake. For all swims off the A66, take the X5 and alight on the minor road which runs through Thornthwaite village, near the junction with the A66. Take extreme care crossing the A66.

For the eastern shore you need the X4 which runs along the A591. Alight at Dodd Wood for a lovely walk to Scarness Bay via Mirehouse and St Bega's Church (2 miles).

All parking is mentioned in the location descriptions.

Refreshments
With the exception of the Pheasant Inn, near Wythop Mill, there are no hostelries right on the lake. The others listed are within a short drive or a nice walk.
- » **Pheasant Inn**, Bassenthwaite Lake. Traditional Cumbrian pub a short walk from Peel Wyke.
- » **Sun Inn**, Bassenthwaite Village. Dog-friendly pub a 1.5-mile walk from Scarness Bay.
- » **Old Sawmill Tearoom**, Mirehouse. Situated a 1.7-mile walk from Scarness Bay.
- » **Middle Ruddings**, Braithwaite. This country inn and restaurant is a short drive from Bassenthwaite Lake.
- » **Braithwaite Village Shop**. Fresh takeaway sandwiches made to order, pies and picnic supplies.

General notes on Bassenthwaite
Bassenthwaite Sailing Club own the rights to boating on the lake and no motorboats are allowed (with the exception of their rescue boats and very occasional survey boats). Races are generally held on Thursday evenings from 7.00 p.m. to 8.00 p.m., on Saturday afternoons between 2.30 p.m. and 6.00 p.m. and Sundays between 11.30 a.m. and 4.00 p.m. The annual regatta is held in the first week of August every year. Check their website for more details of club activities and a webcam showing live weather conditions. Permits to launch boats are available from Keswick Information Centre. *www.bassenthwaite-sc.org.uk*

Opposite Blackstock Point

DERWENT
WATER

Opposite Mid-lake mist in early autumn   **Overleaf** Ian and Tim find things a wee bit chilly at Calfclose Bay

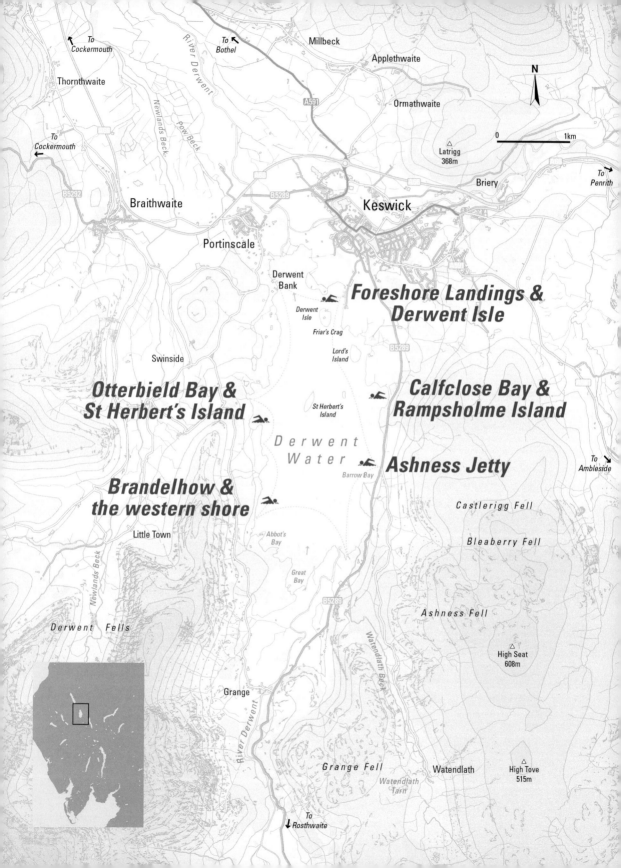

To Cockermouth

River Derwent

To Bothel

Millbeck

Applethwaite

Thornthwaite

Newlands Beck

Pow Beck

Ormathwaite

A591

N

Latrigg
368m

0   1km

To Cockermouth

B5292

B5289

Keswick

Briery

To Penrith

Braithwaite

Portinscale

Derwent
Bank

**Foreshore Landings &
Derwent Isle**

Derwent
Isle

Friar's Crag

Swinside

Lord's
Island

B5289

**Otterbield Bay &
St Herbert's Island**

St Herbert's
Island

**Calfclose Bay &
Rampsholme Island**

Derwent
Water

Barrow Bay

Ashness Jetty

To Ambleside

**Brandelhow &
the western shore**

Little Town

Abbot's
Bay

Castlerigg Fell

Bleaberry Fell

Great Bay

Derwent   Fells

Newlands Beck

B5289

Ashness Fell

High Seat
608m

Grange

River Derwent

Watendlath Beck

Grange Fell

Watendlath

High Tove
515m

Watendlath
Tarn

To
Rosthwaite

Introduction

Jude and Ailie are redoubtable mainstays of Derwent Water. They swim in any weather and at any time of year. Wander down to the boat landings at first light and you will invariably find them on their way to their early morning swim; Jude's laugh ringing out across the water and Ailie sipping hot lemon from a flask, the dogs trotting behind. There are no selfies and no Strava. No posts to Instagram or Facebook. They just swim. It is their morning routine of many years, riding out fads as they come and go.

It was Jude who transformed me from a summer dipper to an outdoor swimmer. She took me for my first 'proper swim' in Derwent Water and it changed the way I looked at water forever. Living in Keswick at the time, Derwent Water was a short walk from home and where I swam most often. We swam loops to the islands and held sunset barbecues, took quick dips to purge a day in the office and delighted in morning light seeping through trees lining the shore. Even swimming the same line day after day I never grew tired of the view.

A bustling tourist magnet, Derwent Water and its hub town Keswick have been attracting visitors for centuries. Early tourists were inspired by the Lake Poets and guided by precise itineraries to dedicated viewpoints.

Eccentric landowner Joseph Pocklington purchased Derwent Isle in 1778 and held mock battles on the water, firing a cannon from his fortified mansion on the island. The Lodore Hotel also owned a cannon and guests could pay for it to be fired across the lake and marvel at the subsequent reverberations around the valley – one of the earliest tourist attractions in the Lake District.

Swimmers today don't need to worry about flying cannonballs. The popularity of Derwent Water has never waned and the lake is very busy during the day. Nowadays it's the frequent launches and pleasure boats that swimmers need to watch out for. Swims in Derwent Water are planned with one eye on the boat timetable.

I treasure the opportunities to swim in Derwent Water at its most spectacular moments. Swimming first thing, before the world comes to life, has been my preference since that first swim with Jude and Ailie, turning me from a night owl to committed early riser.

From nuclear sunrises and balmy sunsets to baltic misty mornings and biting winter winds, it's my lake for all seasons. These conditions are not unique to Derwent Water but the memory of experiencing them in the water for the first time will stay with me in the same way my first mountain sunrise does. Derwent Water is a lake of many firsts for me and will forever hold a very special place in my heart.

1 The original lady of the lake, Jude Gale © Stuart Holmes   **2** Blencathra behind Derwent Water
3 Derwent Water   **4** Looking south into Borrowdale

Foreshore Landings & Derwent Isle

I wouldn't normally advocate swimming from or near a boat jetty, but I make an exception for the foreshore on Derwent Water. It's where my love of open water was born and who am I to deny this pleasure to another hopeful swimmer? During the day it's busy with pleasure boats but arrive first thing in the morning and you will have the place to yourself. Early mornings are my favourite time to swim down the channel towards Friar's Crag. Light falling on the fells is an ever-changing show through the seasons and I could swim up and down this route a hundred times and never get bored.

Although the boats do not tend to launch until after 9.15 a.m. be aware that the residents on Derwent Isle can come across to the 'mainland' in a small motorboat at any time of day.

Derwent Isle is a delight. It lies less than 150 metres from shore, a swim low in effort but one that crosses the path of the launch and other boats. I love to swim round it on a summer's evening, wondering what it would be like to live in the manor house and how they get the stripes on the sloping lawn so neat. Stately Skiddaw forms the perfect backdrop to this swim.

1 Sunrise on Causey Pike   **2** Frosty grass   **3** Back behind the velvet rope ladies, they're spoken for
4 Tim regretting wearing his knee-length wetsuit   **5** Frosty leaf   **6** Cumbria's own David Hasselhoff

Calfclose Bay & Rampsholme Island

I have a love–hate relationship with Calfclose Bay. I've tried to stride purposefully across the pebble shore, after all how much can a few stones hurt? Quite a bit actually. I curse my way into the water, gratefully plunging in as soon as the shelving edge is reached. Once submerged, all is forgiven. It's a perfect treat to starfish in the water and gaze up at Great Wood clinging to the vertiginous face of Walla Crag.

Calfclose Bay is scooped out of the land and sheltered by the peninsula to the north, affording some shelter on windy days. In spring the smell of wild garlic wafts across the bay, carried on a breeze from Rampsholme Island. The island takes its name from one of the many names for wild garlic – 'ramps', but is a slight confusion with the American variety (*Allium tricoccum*) which are commonly known as ramps. It's actually the European *Allium ursinum* known as wild garlic or ramsons that carpet the small island. 'Ramps holme' literally means 'Garlic Island' (*holmr* is Old Norse for small island). That's my kind of island!

If you decide to swim out to Rampsholme Island from here be aware that you cross the route of the launch. The island is roughly 550 metres from the shore.

1

Ashness Jetty

Breaking my jetty rule again, Ashness Jetty is another favoured evening swim spot. There are steps straight down from the road to a sheltered pebble beach with a lovely outlook. Swim here for Cat Bells sunsets and evening light on Falcon Crag; it's under 250 metres in height but it looms like a monolith above the water. Ashness Jetty is probably the easiest swimming location to reach by public transport. The Borrowdale Rambler (78) stops just past the the top of the steps.

Brandelhow & the western shore

While the eastern shore is somewhat over-shadowed by the busy Borrowdale Road, the western shore is much quieter. The road on this side is further away and parking is limited so most traffic is of the pedestrian variety. I don't have a definitive recommendation as the entire shore offers much interest in its rocky beaches and bays.

A walk and swim along the Brandelhow shoreline is a journey through history. This was the first piece of land purchased by the National Trust in the Lake District. Going back even further, the spoil heaps of Brandelhow Bay are relics of sixteenth-century mining. Cat Bells was mined extensively for silver, lead, copper and graphite by German miners brought to Cumbria by Elizabeth I and fenced mine shafts can be seen in this area. Watch your step.

Otterbield Bay & St Herbert's Island

The narrow promontory at the edge of Otterbield Bay is a good starting point for swims to St Herbert's Island. The lakeshore path goes over the top of the headland and few people deviate from it, so the beach below is often quiet. There is pleasant shingle on the beach and some shelter beneath the fractured headland. Otterbield Island is roughly 150 metres from the shore. It's a popular nesting site which we found to our cost as we were dive-bombed on our approach by angry gulls. Swimming to Otterbield Island and then St Herbert's Island is around 650 metres (one way). There is plenty of interest to explore on St Herbert's Island and it's a frequent stopping point for canoeists and kayakers. Swimming to St Herbert's Island involves crossing the path of the launch. The launch will be easily visible from the north but not from the south. Check the timetable before you swim.

1 Otterbield Bay **2** Ashness Jetty

Technical information

MAXIMUM DEPTH **22 metres**   AVERAGE DEPTH **5.5 metres**   LENGTH **2.88 miles**   MAXIMUM WIDTH **1.19 miles**
PRIMARY INFLOWS **River Derwent, Watendlath Beck**   OUTFLOW **River Derwent**

Getting there

The lake is a short walk from Keswick town centre; the foreshore landings are 900 metres from the Moot Hall. Calfclose Bay is a further mile.

Keswick is served by nearly all the bus routes across the region, the principal ones being the 555 from Lancaster via Kendal, Windermere and Grasmere and the X4 and X5 between Workington and Penrith. The 554 comes from Carlisle via Wigton and Bassenthwaite.

The Honister Rambler (77/77A, Easter to October only) serves the western shore and the Borrowdale Rambler (78) serves the eastern shore. Use the Keswick Launch to get to Ashness, Brandelhow and other locations on the lake. It's a lovely way to see the water, second only to swimming in it. In summer a favourite swim is to take the last launch across the lake and swim back to Keswick.

I strongly advocate the use of public transport for Derwent Water, in particular for the western shore where parking is practically non-existent. During holidays I watch the bus struggling through lines of double-parked cars. With ample buses and a regular launch across the lake, there is really no need to drive.

Refreshments

» **Little Chamonix**, Keswick. Regular readers will be familiar with my pie-based tendencies but I'd easily pass up a pie for one of Ellen's cakes.
» **The Square Orange**, Keswick. A tiny, narrow bar serving pizza and tapas and continental beers. The size of the kitchen has to be seen to be believed. It can get quite cosy and you often find yourself sharing a table – perfect for warming up!
» **Fellpack**, Keswick. The staff all love the outdoors and will happily chat to you about walks, runs or bike rides. Tell them about your swim over cocktails and a burger.
» **Thomasons Butchers and Deli**, Keswick. Be at the door by 8.00 a.m. for the best hot pie in town. Mine's a meat and tattie.

Where to Avoid on Derwent Water

With a path hugging practically the entire shoreline, Derwent Water gives swimmers some of the best access to open water. However, it's worth knowing the handful of places to avoid.

Kettlewell

This beach is a popular point of egress for kayakers. It's OK for a splash and paddle but there are dense weeds close to shore. This shallow corner of the lake tends to catch the detritus of the lake and the water quality is not great.

Abbot's Bay

Designated as a protected wildlife and nesting area. Boats are asked to voluntarily avoid the area and swimmers should do the same.

Strandshag Bay

'The shore of the bay frequented by shags.' Lord's Island is a busy roost for shags and the more frequent cormorants, geese and other waterfowl. Their frequent deposits contribute to the rich, sulphurous silt that lines the shallow and narrow channel of the bay. It's quite gross to swim through, especially when the water is low. Like Abbot's Bay, boats are asked to avoid the area. It's one place I am happy not to swim!

Nichol End Marina and Derwent Water Marina

These two busy marinas in the north-west corner of Derwent Water have sail boats moored all year round and smaller craft hired by the hour. There is an outdoor centre nearby too so there can often be flotillas of schoolchildren out on the lake.

Lakeland Rowing Club at Isthmus

Check their website or Facebook page for regular training sessions but bear in mind that rowers can be out on the lake at any time and they travel backwards at a fair rate of knots. *www.lakelandrowingclub.com*

As Derwent Water is a busy boating lake it is particularly important to follow good practice. Wear a brightly coloured cap – neon colours are recommended over silver or white; the drivers and boathands on the launch say the light reflects on silver, white and blue like water, making you virtually invisible – and take a tow float with a whistle tied on. It is easy to find somewhere to swim away from boats, especially if you are swimming early in the morning or in the evening. Awareness has improved but boaters will not necessarily be looking for swimmers.

ULLS-
WATER

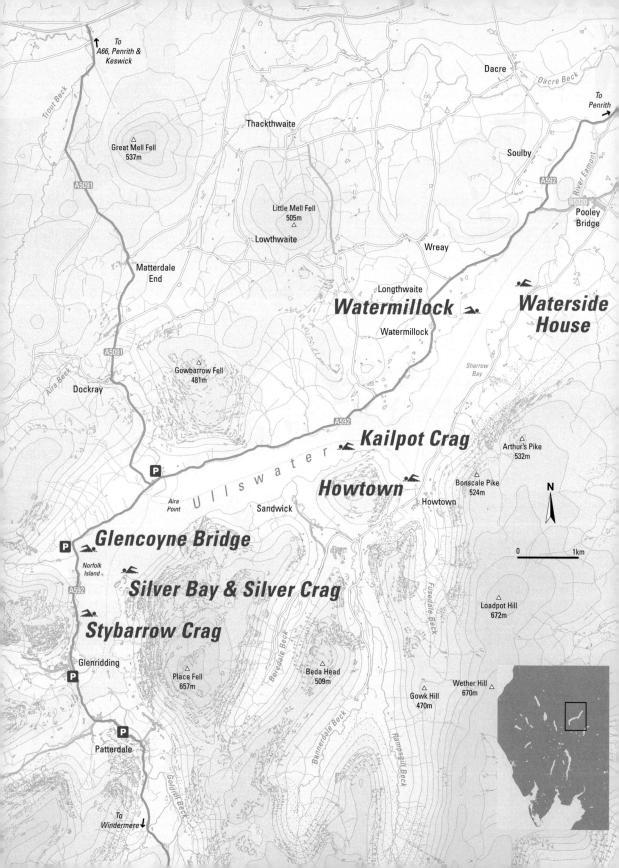

To A66, Penrith & Keswick

Trout Beck

A5091

Great Mell Fell
537m

Thackthwaite

Dacre

Dacre Beck

To Penrith

Soulby

A592

Little Mell Fell
505m

Lowthwaite

River Eamont

B5320

Pooley Bridge

Matterdale End

Wreay

Longthwaite

Watermillock

Watermillock

Waterside House

Aira Beck

A5091

Dockray

Gowbarrow Fell
481m

Sharrow Bay

A592

Kailpot Crag

Arthur's Pike
532m

Ullswater

Howtown

Bonscale Pike
524m

Howtown

P

Aira Point

Sandwick

N

0   1km

Glencoyne Bridge

P

Norfolk Island

Silver Bay & Silver Crag

A592

Fusedale Beck

Loadpot Hill
672m

Stybarrow Crag

Glenridding

P

Place Fell
657m

Boredale Beck

Beda Head
509m

Wether Hill
670m

Gowk Hill
470m

P

Patterdale

Bannerdale Beck

Rampsgill Beck

Goldrill Beck

To Windermere

Introduction

There is something about Ullswater that intimidates me.

I struggle to approach it with the same fond anticipation as Crummock Water, Grasmere or Derwent Water and I can't put my finger on what provokes this unsettled feeling.

Ullswater has claimed the lives of a few people and I put this thought to the back of my mind before a swim. Instead I go through that unspoken risk assessment that every swimmer does, or should do, before I get in. Depth, conditions, entry and exit point, tow float, whistle. I'm acclimatised and warmed up. I have a spotter on the shore or a companion in the water.

Ullswater is less of an old friend and more of an adversary. I prevaricate on its stony shores, lake and swimmer sizing each other up with a shifty eye until I start my watch and take a hesitant step into the water.

The water is slate grey and initially clear, but as you move out it darkens, sucking the light of the sun. Ghostly plant life below the surface looms out of the dark abyss like skeleton hands of hidden beasts desperately reaching for the light. I've swum to Norfolk Island enough times to know the weeds are there, but they wrong-foot me every time.

There is nothing like swimming in the middle of a lake for making you feel completely insignificant. At over seven miles long, Ullswater is the second largest body of water in the Lake District. The vast and dominating Helvellyn range that encloses the head of the lake accentuates my feeling of smallness against the height and bulk of the mountains.

Two distinct kinks in Ullswater's shape create an optional illusion, particularly from the east, where the lake appears to end at Hallin Fell. It's impossible to stand anywhere on the lake and see both ends. These bends split the lake into three sections, created by three separate glacial events. The visual journey along its length takes you from the high fells to the rolling countryside of the Eden Valley as the lake flows out at Pooley Bridge. With such distinct characters in each section, Ullswater is like several lakes rolled into one.

In my attempts to face this particular, and somewhat irrational, fear I have swum all around the lake in stages, around islands and crossed the deepest section many times. Ullswater still sends a slight shiver down my spine and I emerge feeling somewhat relieved but ultimately satisfied.

I turned to Colin Hill for some Ullswater inspiration. His is a name synonymous with open-water swimming, with marathon and solo channel relays under his belt, as well as organising the long-running Chillswim Coniston End to End event. He now coaches swimmers near his home on Ullswater and has probably clocked up more lengths of Ullswater than any other swimmer. He takes inspiration from Ullswater's varied history and revels in the dramatic scenery, taking the windy conditions in his stride. Colin is proud to call Ullswater his home.

I'd better give it another try.

Stybarrow Crag

Don't let my apprehensions about Ullswater put you off. It is a magnificent lake. The best place to appreciate its majesty is from a narrow strip of pebbled beach beneath the road under the precipitous face of Stybarrow Crag. You are in the heart of the action here, perfectly positioned to admire Place Fell and Helvellyn or swim to the photographers' favourite island, Wall Holm.

Glencoyne Bridge

Reputed to be the most famous poem in English literature, William Wordsworth wrote 'I wandered lonely as a cloud' after seeing the daffodils in Glencoyne Park. You can get a unique perspective of them from the water at Glencoyne Bridge.

Across the road from the handy National Trust car park (parking charge), the water is achingly fresh thanks to Glencoyne Beck tumbling down through east-facing Glencoyne and the appropriately named Seldom Seen.

Glencoyne is a good starting point for an assault on Norfolk Island, noting that to swim from the northern shore means crossing the path of the steamer. It's my favourite swim on Ullswater, specifically for the vantage point it offers of Glencoyne and the middle reaches of the lake. From a distance it can be difficult to pick out Norfolk Island against the backdrop of Place Fell, but as you approach the lime-streaked rocks become clear. Norfolk Island is home to cormorants and red-breasted mergansers. It's a protected nesting site and should be avoided during April and May. Outside of nesting season it is a fascinating place to explore or have a mid-swim picnic.

1

Watermillock to Waterside House

This three-mile arc around the end of the lake provides countless opportunities for a dip. The character of the lake is very different here, edged by a much gentler landscape than the southern reaches, a little less daunting. Pooley Bridge is a good base for explorations. It can all be done on foot with only a brief section of road walking. Although tremendously rocky underfoot, I like the beach near the boatyard just out of the village, favouring the quiet calm of early morning, the silence only broken by the relaxing clink of halyards. Weeds in the shallows tickle my feet as I glide over them. They don't seem to bother me as much as they do in the inky depths at the other end of the lake.

The footpath from Pooley Bridge along the southern shore covers almost a mile of shoreline and several stony beaches. There are clusters of sailboats moored along this edge of the lake so care should be taken when entering the water; however, I have never encountered anything bigger than a kayak here.

Beyond Waterside House Campsite the shore is private until Howtown Wyke, except for a small lay-by just south of the Sharrow Bay hotel where you can step from your car and into the water in three strides.

Howtown & Kailpot Crag

Howtown Wyke is the perfect place to greet the day and swim as the sun comes up over the Eden fells, particularly in autumn for the unmistakable and atmospheric guttural sounds of red deer rutting in Martindale. The bay is used by an outdoor education centre and should also be avoided during the operational hours of the steamer. Save this one for an early morning dip.

A path trundles round the base of Hallin Fell high above the water turning the corner of Geordie's Crag and arriving at Kailpot Crag – a sheer cliff about four metres high. It's popular with thrill seekers who jump into the lake below. If you can muster the courage you are braver than I am. Just don't forget to check the depth of your intended landing point before you leap. If you don't fancy the jump there is much easier access into the water on either side of the crag.

Kailpot Crag has a commemorative plaque dedicated to Lord Birkett, situated just above the waterline. He led the charge against Manchester Corporation Waterworks to prevent Ullswater being turned into a reservoir in 1962. He died a few days after the proposition was defeated. As well as the plaque, Ullswater Yacht Club hold the Lord Birkett Memorial Trophy every year in July. It's a spectacle to watch from the shore and from a very safe distance in the water!

Below Swimmer at Ullswater

Silver Bay & Silver Crag

At Silver Bay beat a path through the bracken to a sheltered quiet beach. Several misleading sheep trods exist delving deep into bracken or soaking moss; however, if you look closely, there is a dry and established way leading down to the lake close to Silver Point. The bay is a typical stony Ullswater beach with a weedy fringe and a gently shelving lake bed. It's a bay you can only get to on foot or by boat so it's likely to be quiet, especially as the way down from the path is not readily obvious and many will pass it by.

Silver Crag offers a superb vantage point above the lake. Beneath is a wide bay and small island called Lingy Holm. A more famous geological feature is Devil's Chimney, a rock face emerging from the lake with several vertical fissures emanating upwards. Little information is available on how the headland acquired the ominous name, but it's said to refer to cold air rising off the lake and entering the fissures, then appearing at the top of the cliff like smoke from a chimney.

Technical information

MAXIMUM DEPTH **62.5 metres**   AVERAGE DEPTH **25.3 metres**   LENGTH **7.3 miles**   MAXIMUM WIDTH **0.63 miles**
PRIMARY INFLOWS **Sandwick Beck, Goldrill Beck, Grisedale Beck, Glenridding Beck, Glencoyne Beck, Aira Beck**
OUTFLOW **River Eamont**

Getting there

The northern shore, that is the one with the road running along it, is served by the 508 bus, which runs between Penrith and Patterdale (and to Windermere in summer), and the 208, which runs between Keswick and Patterdale (seasonal service).

The handful of free parking places along the A592 fill up quickly. Further parking is available in the large village car park in Glenridding (parking charge) and the National Trust car parks (parking charge) at Glencoyne and Aira Force.

In Patterdale there is a small car park (parking charge) owned by The Patterdale Hotel.

There is no parking worth telling you about between Pooley Bridge and Howtown. Using the Ullswater Steamer to get to Howtown and continuing on foot is a much more attractive proposition. You can also use the steamer to travel between Pooley Bridge, Aira Force and Glenridding.

Refreshments

» **Howtown Hotel**, Ullswater. The more remote a cafe or pub, the more charm and value I subliminally attach to it, regardless of how good (or bad) the food is. The Howtown Hotel is worth the trip round or across the lake to sit on their pristine lawn or, more likely, in front of a roaring fire. Check the opening times, especially in low season.

» **Fellbites Cafe**, Glenridding. Anywhere that advertises a fried egg sandwich (with two eggs) as a 'lite bite' on their menu is a clear winner to me. On my last visit there didn't appear to be any smashed avocado on their menu which can only be a good thing.

» **The Travellers Rest**, Glenridding. Tucked away up Greenside Road, I'll always walk the extra few minutes for a pint in the cosy bar.

General notes on Ullswater

Ullswater is a busy boating lake. If you don't intend staying very close to shore then a tow float, whistle and bright cap should be the first things out of your bag. It can often be choppy with the fells creating a funnel effect down the valley and along the lake. You definitely shouldn't swim around piers or jetties during operational hours; exercise caution at other times as there might be private sailings or special events, especially in the summer months.

Events take place on the lake year round. Check the Ullswater Yacht Club website for dates of regattas and races before setting out. *www.ullswateryachtclub.org*

Below Colin Hill leaping from Kailpot Crag © Carmen Norman

I have not included any swims near Patterdale or Glenridding as the shoreline is largely private and boats are launched from here. Residents of the lakeside campsite at Side Farm can access the water straight from the campsite. The campsite offers refreshments for passing walkers but a swim here is strictly for campers.

Between Glencoyne Bay and Gowbarrow Bay there are countless small lay-bys where you can pull in and hop straight in the water. These are too frequent and similar to warrant individual references. The lake bed shelves steeply but is generally boat free close to the shore.

Sadly there have been a number of deaths in Ullswater. Not all of them involved swimmers but the majority were people who had entered the lake with the intention to swim or at least paddle. Anecdotal evidence suggests the higher number of deaths in Ullswater could be related to the relative ease of access combined with the steeply shelving edges. Ullswater is a cold lake, fed in various places by very fresh water that emanates from high north- and east-facing slopes. These tend to get less sun and hold snow the longest after winter fades. The warnings of deep cold lakes are often bandied about but with Ullswater they have proved to be accurate so take extra care.

BROTHERS WATER

Opposite The steep side of Caudale Moor above Brothers Water   **Overleaf** Frozen Brothers Water © James Kirby

Wall End

Latterhaw
Crag

Deepdale Beck

To
Penrith

Goldrill Beck

P

A592

Lingy
Crag

Brock Crags
561m

Hartsop

Hayeswater Gill

**Unnamed
spit of land**

*Brothers
Water*

N

Kirkstone Beck

Hartsop Hall

Dovedale Beck

A592

Kirkstonefoot

0   500m

Hartsop Dodd
618m

Pasture Beck

To
Windermere

Introduction

Ask a child to draw a mountain scene and the chances are they will draw a couple of smooth pyramid slopes, perhaps with a dusting of snow on top. Nestled at the foot of the steep-sided Dovedale and Hartsop valleys, the setting of Brothers Water bears a striking resemblance to a child's drawing. The elegant peaks soar above the water, belying their modest heights. The route to the top is as steep as any of the high ground across the Lakeland fells.

Here the tarn or lake argument rears its head. Brothers Water has all the qualities of a tarn but the situation of a lake. Of all the recognised lakes it is definitely the smallest and as tarns go it is smaller than several found higher up in the fells. A swim here has all the qualities of a tarn dip without the effort of a big hike up a hill. Let's stick with calling it a water!

Originally called Broad Water, the name was changed in the nineteenth century in memory of two brothers who drowned here. In the course of my research I came across an incredibly detailed account written by Raymond Greenhow in his blog *Scafell Hike*. His account does the tale far more justice than I ever could, and his blog is well worth a look if, like me, you are fascinated by obscure historical information about Cumbria. *www.scafellhike.blogspot.com*

Nearly and quite neatly square in shape you can walk round Brothers Water in less than an hour. Despite its relatively shallow depths the water is generally cool, being fed straight from the fells. It was once twice the size, although not in living memory. From the concrete lonning (Cumbrian dialect meaning 'lane') between Hartsop Hall and Sykeside Camping Park the damp wetland plain is obvious, long since filled in by debris washed down from Dovedale Beck, Kirkstone Beck and Caudale Beck.

For its tiny acreage, Brothers Water supports a large amount wildlife which is relatively uncommon for a lake of this size. This has led to it being selected as a Site of Special Scientific Interest (SSSI). The designation shouldn't prevent you swimming unless you are disturbing the factors that warrant the SSSI status. In particular, these are botanical features and breeding grounds of a diverse number of bird species. Brothers Water is also home to the schelly, a very rare and endangered freshwater fish only otherwise found in Ullswater, Haweswater and Red Tarn.

Don't forget your snorkel.

Opposite Frozen Brothers Water © James Kirby

Brothers Water benefits from a Miles without Stiles footpath along its western shore. The way into the water isn't as easy, with tricky boulders underfoot on the first and most obvious way into the water, a gravel beach not far from the car park. On one swim with friends Emma and Paul, in an attempt to avoid the rocky lake bed, we waded Goldrill Beck almost to our waists only to encounter a banked lip at the mouth of the beck that we had to step over, finding ourselves back at ankle height in the lake proper.

Further down the path is my preferred place to swim. A grassy peninsula where you can step immediately off the path or continue on the path to the end of the meadow and turn to come back on yourself for step-free access. There is a narrow shingle beach where the water is ankle deep before shelving downwards suddenly into sediment and weeds. There is a slight current here, one of the few places I really notice one. Dovedale Beck, Caudale Beck and Caiston Beck feed into Kirkstone Beck to supply the lake with a steady flow of fresh cool water and it runs along this shore. The movement of water is noticeable, but you are unlikely to be swept down the beck into Ullswater.

1 Not a reliable method of checking the temperature   **2** Breaking the ice © James Kirby
3 A reliable method of checking the temperature © James Kirby   **4** Looking south across Brothers Water © James Kirby

You should avoid swimming close to the reed-fringed southern shore; it's one of the reasons that Brothers Water is an SSSI and is an important nesting ground for many species of bird, notably red-breasted merganser, teal, coot, sandpiper, snipe and cute little dippers. When aquatic life awakens from hibernation and starts to bloom I turn my attentions elsewhere to avoid disturbing the delicate flora and fauna. Swimmers are unlikely to be bothered by fishermen on the water. No permit is required to fish here – often an indication of how poor the fishing is. Boats are not allowed on Brothers Water.

It would be a crime to visit Brothers Water and not walk all the way round. It's a pretty little walk taking in broadleaf woodland and passing Hartsop Hall, a sixteenth-century farmhouse. A concrete lonning links Hartsop Hall to Sykeside Camping Park and then the path continues along the lake, hugging the wall beneath the road. On this side of the lake mature oak, hazel and ash all overhang the water and lilies spread from the eastern corner.

Technical information

MAXIMUM DEPTH **16 metres**   AVERAGE DEPTH **6.2 metres**   LENGTH **740 metres**   MAXIMUM WIDTH **400 metres**
PRIMARY INFLOW **Kirkstone Beck**   OUTFLOW **Goldrill Beck**

Getting there

Brothers Water is served by the 508 bus (seasonal service), which runs between Penrith and Windermere, although this may be subject to local weather conditions on Kirkstone Pass if travelling from the south. Check before you travel as snow and ice can affect the route well into April. This bus operates between railway stations.

For experienced cyclists the approach over Kirkstone Pass, the highest road pass in the Lake District, is undoubtedly tough and absolutely thrilling. An easier, longer approach is from Glenridding and Patterdale as well as a bridleway between Side Farm and Deepdale Bridge.

Parking is available in the small free Lake District National Park car park at Cow Bridge.

Refreshments

» **Brotherswater Inn**, Patterdale.
A traditional, welcoming pub at the foot of Kirkstone Pass, the glowing lights of which guided me back from my second (accidental) benighting on a Lakeland fell. I've never drunk a pint so fast or so gratefully. They also have an extensive whisky shelf and serve hearty meals.
» **Sykeside Camping Park**, Patterdale.
The campsite is dog friendly and open all year round; it has a small shop (seasonal opening). The **Barn End Bar** (seasonal opening) is part of the campsite.
» **The Kirkstone Pass Inn**. Although it's over 280 metres above Brothers Water and nearly three miles away, the chance to combine a swim in the smallest lake with a pint in the highest pub in Cumbria is unmissable.

47

GRAS-MERE

Opposite & Overleaf Autumn sunrise on Helm Crag

N

To
Keswick

Grasmere

Grey
Crag

Lord
Crag

B5287

🅿

🅿

Town End

Wray Gill

Kelbarrow

0   500m

The Wyke

The
Lea

Grasmere

Eastern shore

🅿

🅿

Nab
Cottage

To
Rydal
→

Hunting Stile

Dale End

**Penny Rock
Wood**

Rydal   Water

**Loughrigg
Terrace Beach**

River Rothay

Loughrigg Terrace

Dow
Bank

Introduction

With its central location and inextricable link to William Wordsworth, Grasmere is probably the busiest village in the Lake District. It is a key stop on many a tour itinerary of the Lake District, drawing visitors by the coachload for the cultural history as well as the views. The surroundings might lack the stature and grandeur of Buttermere or Ullswater, but Grasmere more than makes up for that with pretty paths through dreamy broadleaf woodlands all beneath miniature craggy hills. The picturesque setting is effortlessly beautiful, complemented by a perfect chocolate box village. Though busy, you can still find a quiet corner to yourself if you know where to look.

Grasmere and its smaller neighbour Rydal Water are two of the shallowest lakes in the Lake District. The water here tends to be amongst the first to lose the chill of winter and stays relatively mild well into autumn. Fed predominantly by the River Rothay and Wray Gill the water is soft and tea-coloured in the depths.

My favourite time to swim in Grasmere is when the chill of autumn is descending. I love the first view of the lake as I approach from the north over the top of Dunmail Raise. It is nestled in a hollow of low fells and often holds early morning mist on top of the water making for a wonderfully atmospheric dip. You might see fishermen lining the shore near the road, or Martin from Banerigg Guest House striking out for his daily swim from his private jetty.

The watershed above Grasmere is made up of much older volcanic rocky peaks than the softer, lower sedimentary rock directly around the lake and village. The taller peaks don't hold much sway here though. They are rather distant, and the character of the lake is defined by ancient woodlands that cloak the low fells and surround much of the lake. It makes Grasmere feel quite private. Here the trees take centre stage ahead of the hills and in autumn they steal the show completely.

With the exception of the private land around the north basin (not to mention the swans and weeds – more on these later) there are plenty of easy opportunities for a swim around Grasmere. It always strikes me as a very convivial place to enjoy a dip, whether you fancy an attention-seeking splash from the busy main beach or a surreptitious dip in a wooded bay. The distance out to the island from Loughrigg Terrace Beach is just under 800 metres, giving an opportunity to clock up a reasonable distance or simply enjoy a paddle in the shallows. There is a place for everyone on this little lake.

Opposite Penny Rock Wood

1 Deer Bolt Wood   2 Jetty   3 Blanket weed in the north basin © Suzanna Cruickshank
4 Grasmere   5 Autumn mist   6 View from the eastern shore

Eastern shore

Where the A591 runs alongside the lake there are a couple of small lay-bys; one is shortly after leaving Grasmere village, the other is beyond a sharp bend just past Banerigg Guest House, the latter being the best place for access to Penny Rock Wood. Park up and cross the road to the tarmac footpath along the wall above the lake. In some places you can easily hop over the wall to small beaches and get straight into the water. It's possible to hop over the wall but choose your spot carefully to avoid damaging the wall or landing in dense undergrowth. This section of the lake is also popular with fishermen, especially early in the day, so choose your swim spot carefully to avoid getting tangled in their lines!

Close to Banerigg Guest House is a viewpoint with two wrought-iron benches overlooking the lake. Back in the 1800s there were plans for several houses along this stretch of road, each with its own private jetty or lake frontage. Work commenced on a semicircular terrace viewpoint over the lake but eventually the only house that was built was Banerigg, saving the ancient bluebell wood from being cut down. The viewpoint is still there, with a slender gap in the low wall and a wooden bar across the gap. Climb over the bar to negotiate the slate steps down to the water – there is no beach here and the last step hovers precipitously above the water. It is a unique and committing place for a swim but with a with a superb view of Helm Crag.

1

Penny Rock Wood & Loughrigg Terrace Beach

The path from the southern White Moss car park is a Miles without Stiles route. The compacted stone path along the River Rothay and through a meadow is suitable for all. The continuation into Penny Rock Wood has a steeper incline and stone steps down to the bridge crossing the river to the lakeshore. Loughrigg Terrace Beach is a fine place to swim and paddle to your heart's content. The water is very shallow right up to the weir and you would struggle to get out of your depth in usual conditions. Keep an eye on children around the fast-flowing water on the lip of the weir though.

Understandably, a great and easily accessible beach like this gets quite busy. Penny Rock Wood is much quieter, and you can easily find a sheltered bay amongst the trees to slip unnoticed into the water.

One sunny Monday afternoon I counted twenty or thirty people milling around on Loughrigg Terrace Beach and so continued to a shady narrow strip of beach under the edge of Deerbolts Wood. I had this corner of the lake to myself save for an inquisitive mallard, who swam with me for a short distance. The water is a bit deeper here and the lake bed falls away quickly. Underfoot the stones are on the sharp and angular side and pretty uncomfortable for bare feet.

Continuing round the lake after Deerbolts Wood is around half a mile of very pleasant bridleway. There are plenty of places to take a dip along here. My favourite is next to the tumbledown boathouse, but you can find your own on one of the many little beaches along this stretch.

Roughly half the shoreline is privately owned or inaccessible. To the north the shore is edged by reeds and marsh, beyond that are pastoral fields and Grasmere village. The north-west corner of the lake towards the Faeryland tea gardens is the shallowest part of the lake. It is patrolled by a group of territorial swans, headed by their leader Henry, who do not take kindly to swimmers straying into their patch. You have been warned. Along the northern shore and around the mouth of the River Rothay the lake depth is around two metres, most of which is heavy with silt and blanket weed as I found out on a research swim round the island with friend Wayne. Blithely ignoring the warning signs of rapidly shallowing water with a slightly sulphurous smell, we swam to within fifteen metres of the island and found that we could stand on springy mud. Undeterred we carried on. The water got shallower, and then weedy, until we were swimming through what can only be described as bright green hair. As we churned up the silt, putrid gas was released, smelling like rotten eggs left out in the sun. We tried spreading out away from the island, but it was no use. We were well and truly ensnared in the weed and silt. It was a traumatic twenty minutes or so before we managed to extricate ourselves and swim for home towards Loughrigg Terrace Beach during which time the only words we exchanged were punctuated by some fairly robust swearing.

1 Underwater in Grasmere © Suzanna Cruickshank   2 Grasmere from Loughrigg Terrace Beach   3 Helm Crag

Technical information

MAXIMUM DEPTH **21.5 metres**   AVERAGE DEPTH **7.7 metres**   LENGTH **1,500 metres**   MAXIMUM WIDTH **600 metres**
PRIMARY INFLOWS **River Rothay, Wray Gill**   OUTFLOW **River Rothay**

Getting there

Grasmere is well served by the 555 bus, which runs between Lancaster and Keswick, with frequent buses in peak season. The A591, which is the main road through the Lake District, runs along the eastern edge of Grasmere and you can alight the bus alongside the water. There is ample parking at the two car parks at White Moss; payment is by number plate recognition meters. The car park north of the A591 necess-itates crossing the busy A591 road on a bend. You can walk directly to the lake from the car park south of the A591, and it has dedicated disabled parking spaces and accessible toilet facilities. Further parking is available in Grasmere Village, a short walk from the lake.

Refreshments

» **Faeryland tea gardens** are right on the lake with rowing boats to hire (but no swimming).
» There is an ample choice of hostelries, cafes and pubs in Grasmere village. My favourite is **Lucia's Takeaway Coffee Shop**, a temple of sweet and savoury pastry goodness. **Green's Cafe** caters very well for those with dietary requirements with an extensive gluten-free and vegan menu. A bar bustling with locals is always a good sign – **Tweedies** is recommended for evenings.

General notes on Grasmere

The water is deepest to the south of the island. To the north lie those twin ghouls of swimmer folklore: swans and weeds. Take heed of my ill-fated swim with Wayne, and the trauma that will stay with us forever. The north basin is best viewed … from a boat!

Opposite Autumn gold

RYDAL WATER

Opposite Setting off from the southern shore   **Overleaf** A perfect morning

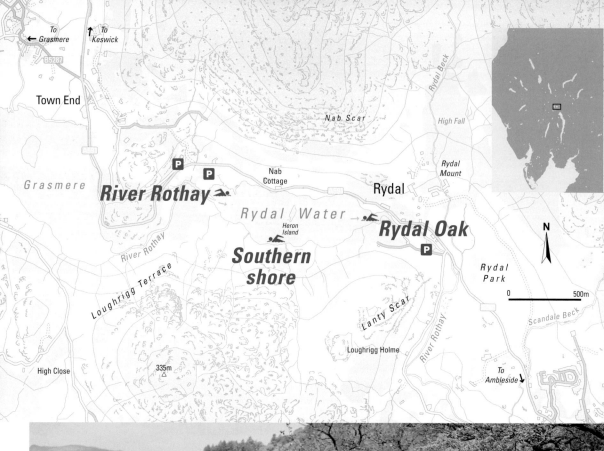

To ← Grasmere

To Keswick ↑

Town End

Nab Scar

High Fall

Rydal Beck

Grasmere

Nab Cottage

River Rothay

Rydal

Rydal Mount

Rydal Water

Rydal Oak

Heron Island

Southern shore

River Rothay

Rydal Park

Loughrigg Terrace

N

Lanty Scar

Scandale Beck

500m

Loughrigg Holme

High Close

335m

River Rothay

To Ambleside ↓

Introduction

Rydal Water is a little gem. It takes all the good things about swimming wild in the Lake District and distils them into one concentrated experience. There is a navigable stretch of river, islands to explore, lakeside paths and craggy fell views. Best of all, in my opinion, it has a terrific pub just across the road for post-swim libations.

Despite the proximity of the A591 along the northern shore I find Rydal Water peaceful and interesting, a real nature lover's lake. Rydal Water has its own pair of swans, vicious man-eating beasts, that patrol the mouth of the river where it enters the lake. Kingfishers flit up the Rothay and frequent the quiet private corners of the north basin. Herons stalk the reed fringes and Canada geese noisily make their presence felt. If you are really lucky, you might see an otter, particularly in the southern reaches.

The twin lakes of Grasmere and Rydal Water share many similar characteristics. They are both shallow, no more than twenty-five metres in the deepest section. Loughrigg Fell sits astride both lakes and offers several pleasant routes between the two on foot or on wheels.

A rare feature for rural Cumbria is an accessible Miles without Stiles path for wheelchair users linking the two lakes and giving access right to the edge of the water.

The River Rothay drains from Grasmere into Rydal Water and in the interests of research I decided to try and swim the river from one lake to the other. I enlisted the help of my friend Anna and we set off, rather drastically overestimating the depth of the river. Defeated after several non-negotiable rocky falls, we slopped along the path to a wide bend further down the river and disrupted the picnic of a conservative-looking family who were spread out on the grass. At this bend the river deepens dramatically – there is a handy sign indicating *DANGER Deep Water*. Here we stepped off a shelf and allowed the gentle current to take us down the short stretch of river, where it is just wide enough to swim side by side. Anna and I glided along, emerging into Rydal through the reeds, the view suddenly opening up in front of us. This remains a highlight of my swimming adventures.

Opposite Strolling towards Rydal Oak

Rydal Oak

My number one place to swim in autumn is where a big old oak tree leans over the water at the end of the lake, its branches reaching out over the surface and autumn gold reflecting on the water. A crag juts out from the shore creating a small, shallow bay that fills with lilies in summer. On the other side of the exposed rock and gnarled tree roots there are several more tall oak trees and a nice patch of grass for picnics. It's off the path and fairly private,

although the road is quite close, just a stone's throw across the mouth of the river. A stone wall shades this changing spot from most traffic, just watch out for snap-happy tourists on the double-decker bus!

Take care immediately after periods of rain which speed up the flow of water leaving the lake here. More than once I've had to chase a wetsuit making a break for freedom this way. It's not enough to sweep a swimmer down to Windermere, and remains shallow enough to stand in, but it might catch out paddlers or small children.

Opposite By the Rydal Oak   **Below** Early morning on Rydal Water

Southern shore

It is a short walk from Pelter Bridge Car Park to the southern shore of Rydal Water, where there are several popular beaches. It's a rare day that you don't see a swimmer here, even in winter. The gently climbing bridleway of compacted stone offers good access to Rydal Water, and on to Grasmere, for those with limited mobility or pushing buggies. The car park is small and fills up quickly but has the added bonus of an ice cream van most days in summer.

The path runs close to the water and you won't be short of an audience. Stepping into the water is initially rocky but it soon deepens. There are four or five islands on Rydal and the two largest are opposite the southern shore, neatly dividing the lake into two basins.

The water is deep enough to navigate between the two main islands (Heron Island and Little Isle) and, outside of nesting season, it is easy to get out and explore. Look out for a ruined hog house and the final resting place of a dog named Crusoe.

River Rothay

One of the pleasures of Rydal Water is how mild it is. Being a small, shallow lake it warms up quicker than most and retains its relative 'warmth' fairly late in the season. A trick to make any lake feel warm is to swim into it via a feeding river.

As previously mentioned, you can swim into Rydal Water from the River Rothay. It's a wonderful safari swim and over far too soon for my liking. As you approach the lake, dense reeds appear to bar your way but there are a couple of exit channels through.

The mouth of the water is shallow and is best avoided after a dry spell as the lake bed is very soft. Disturbing the thick silt releases a sulphurous pong that can leave you eyeing your companions suspiciously.

You should bear in mind that you are committed to swimming at least 400 metres to reach the shore and it's best suited to a one-way trip unless you can swim back up the river against the current. Another advisory is the man-eating swans who nest in the reeds. During nesting season you should give them a very wide berth and avoid disturbing them, but at most other times of year they will merely glide past with a supercilious billow of their wings.

1

Technical information

MAXIMUM DEPTH **18 metres**   AVERAGE DEPTH **5.3 metres**   LENGTH **1,190 metres**   MAXIMUM WIDTH **360 metres**
PRIMARY INFLOW **River Rothay**   OUTFLOW **River Rothay**

Getting there

There are a few car parks within walking distance of Rydal Water. There are two car parks at White Moss (parking charge), one on either side of the A591. The one to the south of the A591 has toilets including disabled facilities and compacted stone paths to Grasmere and Rydal Water. Both car parks are controlled by number plate recognition, pay on exit. The small car park at Pelter Bridge (parking charge) is accessed over a humpback bridge, which may not be suitable for low vehicles.

The car parks fill up quickly and the bus is often the best option – regular services from Keswick via Grasmere and from Ambleside stop at the end of the lane leading to Rydal Hall. Cross the road and cut through the drystone wall opposite the Badger Bar. Access to the water is a short hop over the bridge.

Refreshments

» **Glen Rothay Hotel and Badger Bar**, Rydal. The bar has a hearty menu and great selection of burgers. The rock feature in the toilets is something of a visitor attraction too.
» **Rydal River Cafe**, Rydal. Creative vegetarian and vegan menu served in Rydal Lodge or in the peaceful riverside garden. Signposted from near the river bridge by Rydal Oak.
» **Old School Room Tea Shop**, Rydal Hall. The tea shop serves soups, sandwiches and cake. Take time to walk in the gardens (free entry; donations towards garden maintenance greatly appreciated) or see one of the regular art exhibitions.

1 Ali and Jude in Rydal Water   **2** The view from the old oak tree

ELTER WATER

Introduction

Elter Water is something of a grey area for swimmers. Its situation is undeniably pretty and the backdrop of Great Langdale is much photographed. While researching Elter Water I failed to get a definitive answer on permission for swimming there as the water is privately owned. Plenty of people do swim there though, so I diligently attempted to check it out for myself.

Fed by the River Brathay and Great Langdale Beck, Elter Water reaches a maximum depth of seven and a half metres. It's made up of three mysterious pools, only one of which you can get a good look at as a pedestrian. The swampy fringes make it impossible to get close to the edge of the water. For swimmers, the only realistic entry point is at the mouth of the river where it leaves the largest pool. Limited access is not the only problem facing swimmers in this lake. Beneath the surface, dense elodea (the fancy name for waterweed) bars the way. Then there's a thick layer of silt lining the lake bed which sucks your ankles like quicksand. In short, swimming in Elter Water is not an attractive proposition.

I'm not a fan of wading through mud or silt to get into any water. Not only does it feel desperately unpleasant, I worry I am disrupting the ecosystem and organisms within it. I prefer to leave it be and go elsewhere. I felt Elter Water deserved an explanation, and an excuse to use the photos we took on a cold winter morning. By way of apology to the stoic swimmers Anna, Ben, Emma, Fay, Faye and Sarah who braved the sludge, I have included my research for completists, and for those that won't be told.

Opposite Wetherlam over the River Brathay © James Kirby

For swimmers intent on ticking this lake off their list, the mouth of the largest pool is your best option. The Cumbria Way passes the edge of the pool and you are bound to have an audience here. To negotiate the tricky entrance to the water, try floating forwards and sculling over the worst of it. Out in the middle though, the water is fresh and cool, benefiting from the steady top-up from the River Brathay and Great Langdale Beck.

My attempts to explore the two smaller pools have ended in retreat. The narrow channels are bottlenecks of shallow water edged with reeds, making onward progress difficult. More than once I have come face to beak with a swan and being at eye level with them makes me incredibly reticent to argue. Incidentally, the name Elter Water derives from the Old Norse for 'the lake frequented by swans' and it remains the best place to observe whooper swans as they spend the winter on the lake.

My best experience of swimming in Elter Water was a crisp October morning with Anne and Lottie. We left the Cumbria Way and bushwhacked through undergrowth to reach a channel of the Great Langdale Beck. After wading most of the way we made it to a pebble beach in a northern corner of Elter Water and plunged towards the middle of the lake. One for intrepid swimmers.

Technical information

MAXIMUM DEPTH **7.5 metres**	AVERAGE DEPTH **3 metres**	LENGTH **930 metres**	MAXIMUM WIDTH **400 metres**
PRIMARY INFLOWS **River Brathay, Great Langdale Beck**		OUTFLOW **River Brathay**	

Getting there

Elter Water is on the 516 bus route which runs from Kendal, via Windermere and Ambleside, to Dungeon Ghyll. Alight at Skelwith Bridge and walk just over half a mile north along the River Brathay or alight at Elterwater village and walk half a mile along the Cumbria Way to reach the water. Parking is available at the National Trust car park (parking charge) in Elterwater village.

Refreshments

» **Chesters By The River**, Skelwith Bridge. For post-Elter Water refreshment this is just the ticket, a short walk away along a good path by the River Brathay. It serves a vegetarian menu which is so deliciously creative that this meat-eater did not notice the lack of meat for several visits.

» **The Britannia Inn**, Elterwater village. Traditional pub.

» **The Eltermere Inn**, Elterwater village. For a little more luxury.

General notes on Elter Water

Elter Water is privately owned and permission to swim is not explicit, so if you are asked to leave the water please do so.

1 Their faces belie the terror beneath © James Kirby **2** Lifeguard Rosie at your service © James Kirby **3** Is a swim complete without a brew from an enamel mug? © James Kirby **4** Winter sunrise over Elter Water © James Kirby

WINDER-MIERE

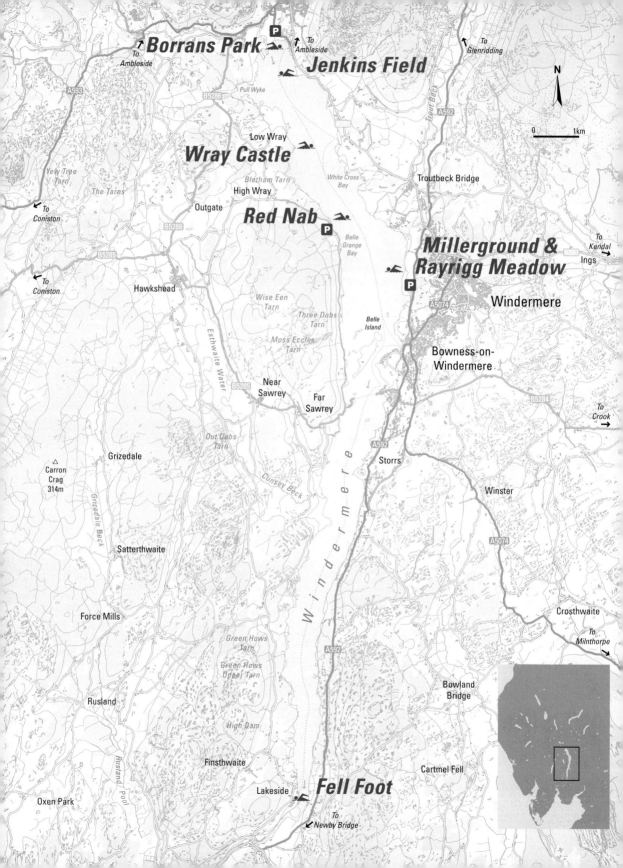

Borrans Park

To
Ambleside

P

To
Ambleside

Jenkins Field

To
Glenridding

Pull Wyke

N

0   1km

Low Wray

Wray Castle

White Cross
Bay

Troutbeck Bridge

Bletham Tarn

High Wray

Yew Tree
Tarn

The Tarns

Outgate

Red Nab

P

To
Coniston

Belle
Grange
Bay

**Millerground &
Rayrigg Meadow**

To
Kendal

Ings

To
Coniston

Hawkshead

Wise Een
Tarn

P

Belle
Island

Windermere

Three Dubs
Tarn

Belle
Island

Bowness-on-
Windermere

Moss Eccles
Tarn

Near
Sawrey

Far
Sawrey

To
Crook

Esthwaite Water

Out Dubs
Tarn

Grizedale

Carron
Crag
314m

Storrs

Winster

Cunsey Beck

Grizedale Beck

Satterthwaite

Windermere

Force Mills

Crosthwaite

Green Hows
Tarn

To
Milnthorpe

Green Hows
Upper Tarn

Rusland

Bowland
Bridge

High Dam

Rusland Pool

Finsthwaite

Cartmel Fell

Oxen Park

Lakeside

Fell Foot

To
Newby Bridge

Introduction

Windermere has long been associated with open water swimming and first hosted the Great North Swim in 2008. Its original base was at Low Wood Bay with 2,200 people swimming in the mile course. The event now takes place over an entire weekend at Brockhole and attracts 10,000 swimmers tackling the six different distances on offer. The Great North Swim has been and continues to be many people's first and possibly only experience of open-water swimming in the Lake District. As the longest lake in England and a qualifying distance for prospective swimmers of the English Channel, Windermere is a siren call for long-distance swimmers.

Since the railway first brought Victorian tourists to a small fishing village on the shores of Windermere, it has been the most popular visitor destination in the Lake District. The eastern shore is predictably busy where the main road hugs the side of the lake pretty much tip to toe. The western shore feels wilder though. It feels different from other parts of the Lake District, with dense broadleaf woodland offering tantalising secretive glimpses of the lake while gnarly mountain scenery is in short supply.

Windermere has a more pastoral setting with the immediate lake edges made up of rolling countryside and woodland, not the crags and precipitous ridges of Ullswater or Wast Water for example. While the Lakeland hills beckon in the distance, it's the lake that really takes centre stage. Gummer's How in the south and Wansfell above Ambleside are lovely low-effort viewpoints where you can really appreciate the majesty of the lake and its stunning 10.4-mile serpentine length. Roughly halfway along the lake is perennial favourite Orrest Head. Alfred Wainwright was so moved by the view from Orrest Head that it inspired him to write his famous fellwalking bibles. I wonder how he felt about swimming.

Despite its well-known association with outdoor swimming, I haven't always found Windermere the easiest place to swim and it was difficult to know where to start. It's the biggest of all the lakes and it can be as busy out on the water as it is in the heart of bustling Bowness-on-Windermere. I swam with local swimmers and chatted with those who know the lake best. Pete Kelly of Swim the Lakes pointed out that where public rights of way exist you can swim anywhere that a path leads to water. All the places to swim are there if you know where to look. So with that in mind, and armed with a map, off I went.

Borrans Park

Best reached on foot (or from the handy car park at Ambleside RUFC), Borrans Park is on the very northern tip of Windermere by Waterhead. It's a short walk from the centre of Ambleside and a peaceful enclave from the madness of the central Lake District in summer. In the park there is a long slate shelter where you will often bump into local swimmers on their lunch break. The shelter would definitely benefit from a row of hooks but as far as changing facilities for the outdoor swimmer go, this is one of the best!

Borrans Park is right on the water and has steps leading down to a shingle beach – watch your step on the last one, it's so high it feels as though the last step is missing. Benefiting from a steady top-up from the River Rothay the water is somewhat fresher than other places on the lake and algae blooms are rarely an issue. Litter is a problem though and I pick glass out of the water on most visits. Mind your step.

A stone's throw across the water from Borrans Park is Waterhead. There are boats moored in the bay, and lake steamers and launches operate from here. Smaller motorised craft and rowing boats are available for hire. Waterhead has a small promenade with cafes overlooking the water. Needless to say, swimming in that direction or from that shore is not recommended. When I launch from Borrans Park I head west towards Seamew Crag and the interesting shoreline around Brathay where cormorants and goosanders patrol the water.

Jenkins Field

The roadside buildings near Jenkins Field look a little forlorn. Prior to the introduction of a six miles per hour speed limit, this area was busy, and speedboats and jet-skis frequented the bay. With their high-speed activities curtailed, Jenkins Field is now a peaceful peninsula edged with trees rising to an impressive crag viewpoint towards Langdale.

Across the road is Stagshaw Garden, another peaceful antidote to this busy part of the Lake District. In spring the woodland floor is carpeted with bluebells and wild garlic and the garden is home to the 57.8-metre Skelghyll Grand Fir, reputedly the tallest recorded in England. The gardens are owned by the National Trust and are free to wander round – great for non-swimming companions or as a warm-up after a chilly swim.

Millerground & Rayrigg Meadow

At the crack of dawn, the lay-by on Rayrigg Road fills up with cars. By 8.00 a.m. they have gone, and as rush hour begins it's as if they were never there. Millerground is where bleary-eyed swimmers from across South Cumbria and beyond meet for an early morning swim. I love swimming here not for the location – it's completely out of my way and inconvenient – but for the lovely group of people I meet when I come here. It's an unofficial group with a strong 'swim at your own risk and stay within your own capabilities' policy.

Swimmers tend to congregate at Millerground. Rayrigg Meadow is a family friendly location a stone's throw to the south, benefiting from a wheelchair and buggy-friendly path from the car park to the lake, a kids play area and accessible toilets.

Fell Foot

Fell Foot is a neatly manicured country park at the foot of Windermere, run by the National Trust. For just £2 you can get a day pass which enables you to change in the luxury of a heated changing room and enjoy a hot shower after your swim. By its very nature outdoor swimming is often less than friendly for swimmers with a disability, but Fell Foot goes a long way to redress the balance. Here you will find wheelchair-friendly paths, a Changing Places facility – the first in the national park – and a free-to-hire all-terrain wheelchair.

Dedicated slipways make it much easier to get in the water and although the lake bed is soft and stony and doesn't shelve you should still enter with care. Non-swimmers can watch from the picnic benches or the comfort of the cafe making this a very family friendly place to swim.

Red Nab

Red Nab is a small wooded National Trust car park (parking charge). Its secluded location on the western shore is a dead end for vehicles and one of the quieter places on Windermere. It is a great starting point for swimming adventures on the western shore.

Wray Castle

My only swim here was a memorable one thanks to a low mist hanging over the lake on a muggy August evening. As the mist thinned and lifted the busy lights of Bowness-on-Windermere briefly appeared from across the lake before grey swept back with a vengeance. The craggy shoreline is thick with overhanging trees and vibrant heather; surrounded by mist it felt quite otherworldly. In clear conditions you have a duck's-eye view of the bustle on the eastern shore, while suspended in soft, moss-green water. A great place to watch the world go by. Wray Castle is a National Trust property; parking is available at the castle (parking charge).

1 Aleks and Wayne at Fell Foot © James Kirby   2 Cumbrian rain © James Kirby   3 Swimmer nutrition © James Kirby
4 Fell Foot © James Kirby   5 Borrans Park © James Kirby   6 Jenkins Field © James Kirby

Technical information

MAXIMUM DEPTH **64 metres**   AVERAGE DEPTH **21.3 metres**   LENGTH **10.4 miles**   MAXIMUM WIDTH **0.99 miles**
PRIMARY INFLOWS **River Brathay, River Rothay, Trout Beck, Cunsey Beck**   OUTFLOW **River Leven**

Getting there

Unless you are travelling outside normal working hours or not in peak season expect roads to be busy with local and tourist traffic. Windermere is one of the best-served lakes for public transport; on foot or by bus is often the most convenient way to get around. Bike hire is available within a short walk of the bus and railway station in Windermere village from Total Adventure Bike Hire and Country Lanes Cycle Centre.

Stagecoach buses operate along the eastern shore. The number 6 operates a limited service between Windermere railway station and Barrow-in-Furness calling at Bowness-on-Windermere Ferry Pier, Fell Foot and Newby Bridge. The 555 (Kendal to Keswick) serves the north of the lake and the 599 operates between Bowness-on-Windermere and Grasmere. The 505 shuttles between Windermere and Coniston via Hawkshead and Ambleside. If you are arriving from further afield, Windermere is linked via regular services from Keswick, Penrith, Kendal, the southern Cumbrian peninsulas and Lancashire.

Windermere Railway Station is the terminus for the single branch line service that offers connections with the West Coast Main Line and Manchester Airport.

A quaint chain ferry crosses the lake between Bowness-on-Windermere and Far Sawrey. If you find yourself in Bowness-on-Windermere and wanting to be in Hawkshead, or vice versa, the ferry is the quickest way across.

Refreshments

» **Homeground**, Windermere village. I love a good breakfast after an early morning swim and Homeground is a royal treat. They only serve breakfast and brunch, along with good coffee and cake.
» **Method @ Fell**, Kendal. This comes recommended by local swimmers who travel from Kendal to Windermere for early morning dips.
» **1st Floor Cafe**, inside Lakeland, Windermere village. Not an obvious choice, but the combination of a lovely cafe and the opportunity to browse the Tupperware in the shop downstairs is weirdly compelling. Best for home and kitchen gadget fetishists.
» **Bandito Burrito**, Windermere village. This spicy Mexican street food makes a refreshing change to twee Lake District coffee shops. I save this as a winter treat as my palate is hopelessly unaccustomed to spice.

1 Rayrigg Meadow   **2** Borrans Park © James Kirby

CONISTON WATER

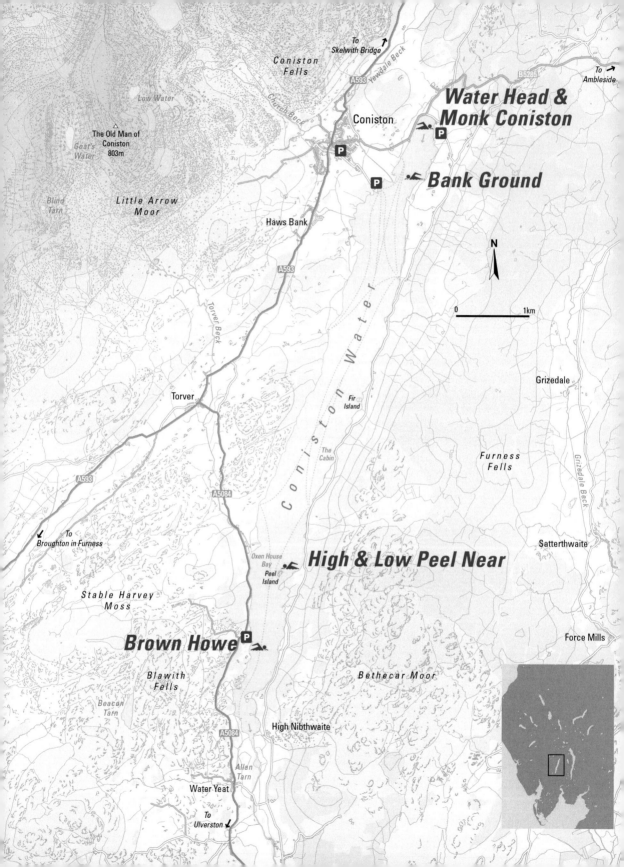

Coniston Fells

To
Skelwith Bridge

Yewdale Beck

A593

To
Ambleside

B5285

**Water Head &
Monk Coniston**

Low Water

Coniston

P

P

Bank Ground

The Old Man of
Coniston
803m

Church Beck

Haws Bank

Goat's
Water

N

Blind
Tarn

*Little Arrow
Moor*

A593

0   1km

Coniston Water

Torver Beck

Grizedale

Torver

Fir
Island

*Furness
Fells*

Grizedale Beck

The
Cabin

A593

A5084

Satterthwaite

To
Broughton in Furness

Oxen House
Bay

*Stable Harvey
Moss*

High & Low Peel Near

Peel Island

Force Mills

Brown Howe

P

*Blawith
Fells*

Bethecar Moor

Beacon
Tarn

High Nibthwaite

A5084

Allan
Tarn

Water Yeat

To
Ulverston

Introduction

Stretching ribbon-like for over five miles, Coniston Water is a true summit-to-sea lake. Its source rises in the high fells enclosing Coniston village; the outflow is the River Crake which joins the coastal estuary of the River Leven at Greenodd five miles to the south.

Coniston Water is slightly separated from the rest of the Lake District in a way that no other lakes are. Its hills and high ground do not form any continuous ridges or links to other groups of hills and the entire area is neatly encircled by roads. The roads form a border in more ways than one. Historically, Coniston was part of Lancashire until the area was absorbed into the new county of Cumbria in 1974.

Donald Campbell, John Ruskin and Arthur Ransome are names synonymous with Coniston Water. Admittedly, the high-speed record-breaking exploits of Donald Campbell are perhaps less relevant to swimmers, although some might find macabre interest in swimming his route and lingering at the crash site that claimed his life. Watching the sedate steamers sailing by, it's pretty hard to imagine anything travelling over 250 miles per hour on this lake. However, each November the ten miles per hour speed limit is temporarily relaxed for the annual Coniston Power Boat Records Week. Swimmers beware.

Celebrated thinker John Ruskin was well travelled across the globe, but he chose to make his home on the shores of Coniston Water. He favoured mountains more by 'the beauty of their glens than the height of their summits'. In this respect, Coniston Water was the absolute best choice for him. Ruskin found inspiration in the gentle character of Coniston Water and its uniformly slender shape. Like Windermere, the mountain scenery is contained to the head of the lake and the landscape softens as it flows south.

If I could only ever do one swim again, the swim to Wild Cat Island (Peel Island) would be in my top ten. I didn't have a *Swallows and Amazons* childhood and came to Arthur Ransome's work as an adult. He picked out locations on Coniston Water and Windermere for his tale, Peel Island being one of the most famous landmarks. It is utterly enchanting to swim into the bay and be dwarfed by its cliffs, evoking a child-like sense of excitement.

Writing Coniston Water has been slightly troublesome. Not only did I lose my entire notes and drafts at a crucial stage, its distance from my base in the north-west Lake District made it easy for me to put Coniston off for another day. I'm indebted to Anna for logistical support, lodgings and a never-ending supply of crisps and cider, and to Edward for sharing his passion and enthusiasm for the lake and helping me appreciate its majesty.

Water Head & Monk Coniston

At the head of the lake, Water Head and Monk Coniston are a calm enclave away from activity. The bigger boats and launches won't trouble you here, but you should still be aware of smaller craft that can be launched from the piers at Coniston Boating Centre.

A narrow stone beach arcs round the bay and, although the road passes close by, it's a nice place for paddling or a lazy dip. In spring this beach is overrun with wild garlic and in autumn the water is flecked gold by falling leaves.

The famous Chillswim Coniston End to End finishes at Monk Coniston. It takes place every September, starting at the southern end of the lake and swimming north, allowing for the most fantastic views as you progress up the lake.

Bank Ground

This section of shoreline is private; however, the owners of Bank Ground are welcoming to swimmers. Bank Ground Farm will be familiar as Holly Howe, the fictional farmhouse in *Swallows and Amazons*. These days it is a bed and breakfast with self-catering cottages and a charming tearoom. Guests are welcome to swim during their stay or on a visit to the tearoom provided that you ask permission first. They even sell tow floats and swim caps in case you have forgotten yours. Swim here for a magical view of The Old Man of Coniston, and a nice slice of cake afterwards.

High & Low Peel Near

High Peel Near and Low Peel Near are two quaintly named peninsulas on the eastern shore. They are eternally popular due to their proximity to Wild Cat Island (Peel Island) so you are best to arrive early, or on foot. The Steam Yacht Gondola stops nearby at Parkamoor. The eastern shore gets the evening sun in summer and swimming around Peel Island as the sun dips down behind Beacon Fell is just glorious.

Low Peel Near is further from Peel Island (around 450 metres) and has a prominent and popular beach. It's lovely underfoot as the shingled shore shelves slowly into the water, but watch out for scattered, submerged boulders lying in wait to trip you up.

If busy, and it often is, wander through the woods of High Peel Near and find your own spot. The small wooded peninsula is crisscrossed with paths all leading to the water. Pick the right path and you will find yourself directly opposite Peel Island which is eighty metres from shore.

Limited parking keeps the eastern shore beautifully quiet, although inevitably the easier to access beaches will be popular in summer. I've picked out High Peel Near and Low Peel Near as key locations to visit but in truth there is a lot to explore between Brantwood and the private Water Park Lakeland Adventure Centre. The real charm of the peaceful eastern shore is the options it offers. Don't take my word for it, go and have a look yourself.

Brown Howe

Brown Howe gives a rare opportunity for swimmers with limited mobility to access the water with relative ease. There is quick, level access from the car park to the shore suitable for wheelchairs and buggies, and there are disabled facilities too. Close to the shore the water is shallow, great for paddling and so smooth underfoot it's as though some kind soul has landscaped the area for swimmers.

1 & 2 Brown Howe © James Kirby **3** Low Peel Near
4 Heading for Peel Island **5** *Swallows and Amazons* secret harbour **6** Monk Coniston © James Kirby

Technical information

MAXIMUM DEPTH **56.1 metres**   AVERAGE DEPTH **24.1 metres**   LENGTH **5.2 miles**   MAXIMUM WIDTH **0.45 miles**
PRIMARY INFLOWS **Torver Beck, Church Beck, Yewdale Beck**   OUTFLOW **River Crake**

Getting there

The 505 bus runs from Windermere to Coniston Water via Ambleside and Hawkshead; the X12 bus (Monday–Friday only) runs from Barrow-in-Furness to Coniston Water via Ulverston and Torver.

The main car parks around Coniston Water are at Brown Howe, Monk Coniston and Coniston village; all are pay on arrival.

At Coniston Boating Centre you can park up for the day (parking charge) and hire bikes, paddleboards, canoes, rowing boats and motorboats or take the Coniston Launch or the Steam Yacht Gondola across the lake.

There are several small, free car parks on the eastern shore but they fill up quickly. Park up in Coniston village and take the Coniston Launch or the Steam Yacht Gondola to cross the lake and wander along the shore looking for the perfect swim spot – get off at Brantwood or Parkamoor for the best options.

Refreshments

» **Swallows and Amazons Tearoom**, Bank Ground Farm. Everything is home-made here and meat is reared on the farm. Stop here for a morning swim and breakfast then order a picnic to take away as you explore the rest of the shore.

» **Torver Deli**, Torver. Handy for the south of the lake. Stock up on picnic goodies here – I hear the vanilla slices are good.

» **Our Plaice**, Coniston. Every swimmer, mountain biker and walker said this was the *place* for fish and chips in Coniston, and there was a queue out of the door and round the corner on my first visit – always a good sign. Pie, chips and gravy for me!

» **The Sun**, Coniston. A charming old inn, the kind with a creaky door and warm welcome. Whoever decorated the bar is *very* fond of corny quotes and motivational signs; it's hard to tell if they are ironic or not.

» **The Black Bull Inn**, Coniston. Home to one of the most famous pints in Cumbria, Bluebird Bitter. Named after Donald Campell's boat, it's a fitting post-swim pint and the food is good too.

1 Bank Ground © James Kirby   **2** Brown Howe © James Kirby

DEVOKE WATER

Opposite Fiona at the boathouse **Overleaf** Seat How above Devoke Water

Minor road to
Eskdale Green

High Ground

Rough
Crag

Water Crag

P

Birker Fell

Seat
How

D e v o k e   W a t e r

Boat house

Birkby Fell

Limbeck Gill

Rigg Beck

Hall Beck

Woodend

Minor road to
Ulpha

N

0   500m

Introduction

Every good list should have a wildcard entry. Greatest mountains. Top ten albums. Best chocolate bars. An entry that makes you stop and ponder, one that ensures debates will rage in pubs across the land. Devoke Water is my wildcard for this guidebook. Depending on your point of view, Devoke Water is the biggest tarn in the Lake District, or one of the smallest lakes.

The dividing line between lakes and tarns is arbitrary at best. Their altitude is often a deciding factor as well as size. Many of them, rather helpfully, have tarn in their name, such as Bowscale Tarn or Red Tarn. These bodies of water are miniature lakes in elevated mountainous terrain. They are usually more demanding to get to, although tarns can also be found on valley floors.

Devoke Water is one of the more accessible wild places for non-hillwalkers. Situated half a mile from the steep winding fell road between Eskdale and Dunnerdale, Devoke Water feels a million miles from civilisation, although it feels less wild knowing your car is only ten minutes away. The wild and desolate location is over 200 metres above the Eskdale valley, hidden from sight as you drive along the road. Devoke Water stretches for just over a mile, perfectly proportioned in its sequestered setting. From the middle of the water the view west is unique; the lack of hills in this direction creates an infinity pool effect. On my most recent visit I met an architecture student involved in a project to rebuild the boathouse before it crumbles beyond repair. The plans includes a conversion to holiday accommodation, information I met with slight reservation. The structure is undoubtedly worth saving. I just hope this familiar and much-loved ruin does not become modified beyond recognition and access becomes out of bounds.

Opposite Distant fells beyond Devoke Water

There is a small island in Devoke Water called Watness Coy. Ancient cairns can be found south-west of the water and there is evidence of Bronze Age industry and activity too. Local historians believe the area was an important trade route and small settlement.

The oak trees of this period are long gone, replaced with typical upland vegetation that is often wet underfoot. The dilapidated boathouse at the head of the water adds to the air of solitude and is an obvious pausing point. The area around the boathouse is one of the better locations to launch yourself into the water, a place I favour for sheer simplicity. It's the area you are most likely to have company or an audience though and for not much more effort you can seek out a quieter spot along the fringes of the water.

1 Devoke Water   **2** Seat How and boathouse
3 Underwater light © Suzanna Cruickshank   **4** The boathouse

Devoke Water is often deserted. It's a place to while away a summer's day, somewhere I never hurry home from. After a swim, I relish the grassy pathless walk over the unfrequented tops. These modest hills make for a lovely walk, offering views of the Irish Sea, the Isle of Man and, nearer to home, upper Eskdale, Sca Fell and Scafell Pike.

Devoke Water has a metallic tang to taste; the rusty hues stem from the presence of peat and iron ore in the landscape. Devoke Water is relatively shallow, averaging under six metres, and crisp for most of the year. Those few extra metres of elevation and lack of shelter from stiff coastal breezes see me packing a hot-water bottle and an extra jumper.

4

Technical information

MAXIMUM DEPTH **14 metres**   AVERAGE DEPTH **5.5 metres**   LENGTH **1,160 metres**   MAXIMUM WIDTH **420 metres**
PRIMARY INFLOWS **Rigg Beck, Hall Beck**   OUTFLOW **Linbeck Gill**

Getting there

Getting to Devoke Water does push the limits of including it in the lake category. It's as remote as Wast Water with the added spice of a steep road to climb. There is no public transport to Devoke Water. Cyclists can grit their teeth and tackle the challenging incline and hairpins. Parking is possible for a handful of cars near the crossroads on the verge but don't block the access to High Ground. The ground is rarely dry; vehicles can easily get stuck in wet weather. For walkers, it's a steady trek of nearly three miles from Eskdale, going via Stanley Force for the full tourist experience. Sim's Travel in Eskdale offer a reasonably priced taxi service. Getting a taxi to the road top and then walking back down after a swim is a very civilised afternoon outing indeed.

The Millom and District Angling Association hold fishing rights to the water, so take care not to disturb their activities; there is plenty of room for everyone around the water.

Refreshments

Lonely Devoke Water does lend itself perfectly to a lazy undisturbed picnic. Take a stove (and a torch) and watch the sunset. Then go to the pub on your way home! You will pass the **King George IV Inn** at the road junction on your way up Birker Fell. It's a real spit-and-sawdust-type pub with a huge open fire and decent real ale.

Opposite Last light at Devoke Water

WAST WATER

Opposite The Screes   Overleaf The broken crags of Whin Rigg above the River Irt

Nether Wasdale
Common

Greendale
Tarn

Middle Fell
582m △

N

0   1km

To
Wasdale Head

Lingmell Beck

P

Lingmell Gill

Wasdale Head

Wasdale Head
Hall Farm

Sca Fell
964m △

Overbeck Bridge P

W a s t   W a t e r

Roadside shore

Harding Gill

YHA & Nearby
Beaches

Along
the Screes

Illgill Head
609m △

Burnmoor
Tarn

Eskdale Fell

To
Gosforth

River Irt

Whin Rigg
△ 535m

Tongue
Moor

Eskdale
Moor

Introduction

Being one of those 'iconic' Lake District destinations, Wasdale is much written about. The emphasis tends to fall, quite understandably, on the scale and grandeur of the valley and the lake it encompasses. Wast Water is not just the deepest lake in the Lake District but the deepest in England too. Nearby Scafell Pike is the tallest mountain in England and is surrounded by equally grand satellite fells. It is the central massif of the Lake District from which the trajectory of high terrain extends for miles. Wasdale is the kind of place that can leave you feeling a little bit, well, insignificant.

For motorists at least, Wasdale is a dead-end valley. The road peters out at Wasdale Head and onward travel from here must be self-powered. Visiting the valley requires effort as it is not on the way to anywhere and has no public transport (though rumour has it you can still grab a lift in the post van). As you turn off the A595 at Gosforth on to the winding valley road it can feel like you are leaving civilisation behind and entering a wilderness. There is no mobile signal. They barely have a television signal up at Wasdale Head, and electricity didn't arrive in the valley until the 1970s. Wasdale really is the valley time forgot.

Stark imposing hills enclose the head of the valley, giants in both stature and mountaineering history. Brooding crags bristle with atmosphere. Even in the spring sunshine with lambs gambolling in the fields, there is a slight menace to the mountainous backdrop. Wasdale is mean and moody, with no soft edges and heaps of attitude. I absolutely embrace the extremes of Wast Water. I love the petrifying depth on the edge of the Screes and swim across to sit on submerged ledges and dangle my legs over a void that goes on forever. The Screes reflect grey across the water but beneath the surface the colour is an electrifying cyan blue.

The water is bracingly cold all year round. It's the clearest, purest lake too, supplied by water from becks and streams that rise in the very heart of the Lakeland fells. The cold is like a slap in the face. In summer, having acclimatised to the relative mildness of Bassenthwaite Lake or Derwent Water, I find my swims have lost that endorphin rush of razor-sharp cold water. When this happens I know it is time to head to Wast Water.

Opposite Great Gable

Wasdale Head

At the head of Wast Water there is a National Trust campsite and car park. Access is limited here and, if I'm honest, so is my research. After one benighted swim which featured a four-metre scramble and lots of brambles, and another featuring a very fast river swim resulting in some minor bruising, I resolved that if there was no right of way on foot, I would go elsewhere. If you absolutely must swim from the head of the lake there are ways in either via careful negotiation of Lingmell Beck or Lingmell Gill, from the roadside or from Wasdale Head Hall Farm.

Along the Screes

If you like your water cold and deep then arriving at Wast Water is a good start. If you also like a proper challenge then a 'walk' along the Screes should scratch that particular itch. The shattered boulders of the southern lakeshore are not really considered to be a path, more a boulder field requiring you to hop and scramble from rock to rock – even for the most fleet of foot it will prove slow-going. Where the Screes enter the water they continue beneath the surface, a sheer drop leaving no ledge or lake bed to stand on. A swim of absolute commitment and not for the faint-hearted or inexperienced.

YHA and Nearby Beaches

Wast Water's granite beaches are tough going on bare feet. I've not yet found a way in that doesn't leave me rueing a forgotten pair of swimming shoes, sat uselessly at home. Thankfully, the perma-chill of the water quickly takes my mind off the sharpness of the stones!

A path around Low Wood arrives at the lake near the mouth of the River Irt and continues to a pink granite beach with that classic, endlessly photographed view of pyramidal peaks at the head of the lake. It's just off a footpath but feels like it's just you and the lake. Here, the lake bed gradually shelves allowing a gentle wade in rather than a plunge, unlike the rest of the lake.

The path continues and passes by YHA Wasdale Hall, a grand building dating back to 1829. This hostel couldn't be better situated for a wild swimming weekend, with only a lawn and a small car park separating the building from the lake.

Roadside shore

Not far past YHA Wasdale Hall the path runs out and you find yourself walking on the road or over rough ground. Along these first stretches of road it's easy enough to walk along the shore and dip in wherever an opportunity presents itself. For drivers, there are several lay-bys of varying size affording instant access from car to water. Make sure you are not parking in a passing place! Wast Water is a popular diving location and you will often encounter divers on this stretch of coastline. Along this shore the lake bed shelves quickly and deeply. Non-swimmers and paddlers should take care. Such is the clarity of the water that you can still clearly see the lake bed and feel as though you might graze it with a toe even at a depth of several metres, until it slides off into a great void. Swimming in Wast Water is the closest I will ever get to flying.

Overbeck Bridge

There is a small free car park at Overbeck Bridge where tingly cold Over Beck flows into Wast Water. It's even colder than the lake! Swim here for a majestic view of Hollow Stones, Pikes Crag and Scafell Pike.

1 Overbeck Bridge   2 Underwater at the Screes © Suzanna Cruickshank   3 Overbeck Bridge with Lingmell Gill behind
4 Near the YHA beach   5 Underwater at the Screes © Suzanna Cruickshank   6 Near the roadside shore

Technical information

MAXIMUM DEPTH **76 metres**   AVERAGE DEPTH **39.7 metres**   LENGTH **3 miles**   MAXIMUM WIDTH **0.51 miles**
PRIMARY INFLOWS **Nether Beck, Over Beck, Lingmell Beck, Lingmell Gill**   OUTFLOW **River Irt**

Getting there

There is no public transport to Wasdale. The closest you can get by bus is on the Borrowdale Rambler (78) from Keswick; alight at Seatoller to hike over Sty Head Pass – it's a magnificent three-hour walk in mountainous terrain. Trains run along the west coast of Cumbria and stop at Seascale, Drigg and Ravenglass – convenient in the loosest sense of the word, it will require self-power or a taxi booked in advance to complete the journey.

The valley road runs along the length of the lake; there is a small car park at Overbeck Bridge (payment by donation) and further parking at the National Trust car park at Brackenclose (parking charge).

Refreshments

» **The Screes Inn** and **The Strands Inn**, Nether Wasdale. These two pubs serve a wide variety of food (The Screes Inn has plenty of vegetarian and vegan options); best of all they share their own microbrewery.

» **Wasdale Head Inn**, Wasdale Head. One of the most remote pubs in the Lake District situated at the road end at the head of the valley.

» **Gosforth Bakery**, Gosforth. Purveyors of pies of mythical stature. The bakery closes at 2.00 p.m. if not earlier – avoid disappointment and buy your pies on the way to the lake!

General notes on Wast Water

Small patches of mobile phone signal and 4G have started appearing in Wasdale but it should be assumed that there is no reliable signal in the valley.

Opposite Sca Fell above Wast Water from Overbeck Bridge

BUTTER–MERE

Opposite Horse Close larches   **Overleaf** Snowy High Crag and Burtness Comb from Pike Rigg

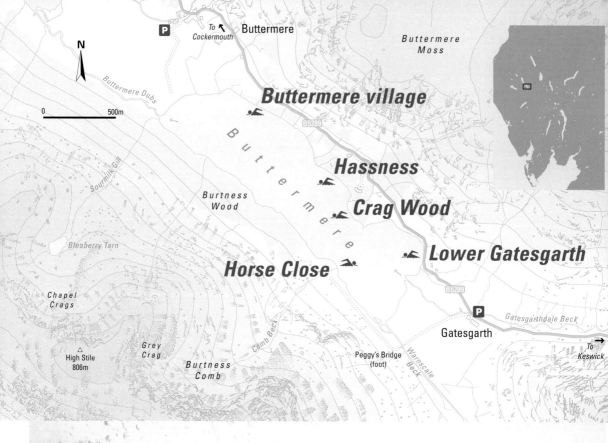

Introduction

Buttermere fills my heart with joy. It's like your favourite song that's only two minutes long and you wish it went on longer. Buttermere is a small lake, but if it was bigger – if you magnified all those things that make it special – it wouldn't be special any more. Bigger doesn't always mean better. The best things in life always leave you wanting more.

What makes Buttermere special, to me and to the thousands of visitors each year, is how much is crammed in to a relatively small valley. Buttermere is just over a mile in length; a circuit of the lake by the charming lakeshore path can take less than a couple of hours. Its sylvan charm is complemented by the towering tops of Red Pike, High Stile and High Crag, which can be reached in a similar amount of time, although requiring an entirely different level of effort. When it comes to the reward-for-effort ratio, Buttermere lake and valley offer unparalleled value for money and adventure for all abilities.

Set in a similar geological landscape to Wast Water, Buttermere is just as dramatic below the surface as above.

The lake is fed by becks and streams running straight down from high fells surrounding the lake. The water has little time to warm up before it reaches the lake, rendering Buttermere crisp and cool all year round despite the relatively shallow maximum depth of around twenty-eight metres. Its edges are precipitous in places, particularly along the eastern and western shores which, for me, just adds to the thrill of swimming here.

I've been lucky enough to live within a twenty-minute drive of Buttermere for more than ten years now. Even so, the first glimpse of Red Pike on the final descent over Newlands Hause never fails to lift my heart. It's the first hill I climbed, and it ignited a passion for this particular part of Cumbria. I have to pinch myself that I can swim here whenever I feel like it. Buttermere will never be a workhorse swim for me. I come here for joy not exercise. The exhilaration of stepping forward into the beckoning teal-blue void never diminishes. Buttermere is a real treat, a four-finger KitKat swim.

Opposite Photographer Stuart gets low to snap Tim and Ali. We think he is still down there © Stuart Holmes

Horse Close

Around the head of the lake is the only part of Buttermere where the path deviates from the lakeshore. It leaves the lake at Lower Gatesgarth and continues briefly on the road before crossing Warnscale Bottom to the quaintly named Peggy's Bridge. The path remains slightly higher than the lake and would require a climb down the rough slope to get to the water. I have never been tempted to swim along this stretch in the knowledge that a favourite location lies not too far ahead. Horse Close, where a clump of larch trees cover a flat peninsula, is directly beneath Burtness Comb. Few walkers deviate off the path here and until recently there was a gate barring the gap in the wall. It is a quiet enclave on busy days. With water crashing down from Burtness Comb it is always slightly fresher around Horse Close and beautifully clear. It is also a great place for a post-swim picnic.

Buttermere village

The track out of the village towards the lake must be one of the busiest foot highways in the Lake District. Endless pairs of boots tramp along here all year round heading for the high fells or a sedate circuit of the lake. And now, increasingly, feet are carrying swimmers along the path towards the edge of the lake. At the final gate the classic Buttermere view appears. A small meadow stands between you and the water. The slope of Fleetwith Pike draws the eye down to the water and Warnscale Head broods magnificently at the head of the lake. Initially the lake bed is unforgiving, paved with awkward rocks. Your steely determination to enter the chilly water barefoot must be matched by steely soles. On a fine summer's day this is a popular spot for family paddling – shoes are highly recommended for splashing about. The lake bed is shallow for quite a distance, some twenty metres or so, however non-swimmers should still be supervised.

1 Light on Horse Close and Hay Stacks behind   2 Buttermere shore

Hassness

For early starts (or late ones) you can park on the road near Hassness and follow a sylvan path along the beck and through the wood. The parking strip fills up during the day but the bus will stop here on request. The small bay is less than a five-minute walk from Crag Wood, but the two locations have entirely different characters and qualities for swimming – this I feel makes them worthy of separate inclusion. Lottie introduced me to swimming here one breezy October day. The beauty of Hassness is how sheltered it is by the headland of Crag Wood. While white horses are whipping across the middle of the lake you will be guaranteed a gentler time here. Overhanging trees obscure the path along the edge of the water as it emerges over a rock step from the Hassness Tunnel; you will almost certainly have some spectators on this swim! There is a bench for non-swimmers to take in the view. A messy tangle of blue pipework right in the middle of the bay is the water supply pipe to the manor house and is easily avoided as you wade in. As with much of Buttermere the swimmable depth is reached after several purposeful strides.

Crag Wood

This narrow spit of fine slate is one of my first and most enduring loves of the Lake District. The peninsula sticks out into the water with a magnificent view of High Stile and High Crag. It is a committing swim. A couple of steps forward and you are floating freely above the edge of the deepest part of the lake. The fine shingle is a joy underfoot. Put your head underwater and marvel at the perfect clarity. The view is exhilarating above and below.

Lower Gatesgarth

Where the road runs close to the lake at Lower Gatesgarth there is a small beach just beneath the embankment. It's rather public but a decent spot to swim from and where I usually set off to swim the length of the lake. The gravel beach is adjacent to the only strip of private lakeshore but I'm sure the landowner won't mind you swimming past to look at the view!

1 Dodd and Burtness Wood across Buttermere   **2** High Crag and High Stile

Technical information

MAXIMUM DEPTH **28.6 metres**   AVERAGE DEPTH **16.6 metres**   LENGTH **1.28 miles**   MAXIMUM WIDTH **0.34 miles**
PRIMARY INFLOWS **Gatesgarthdale Beck, Warnscale Beck, Comb Beck**   OUTFLOW **Buttermere Dubs into Crummock Water**

Getting there

Leave your car and take the Honister Rambler (77/77A), Easter to October only, from Keswick. It is a fantastic journey.

Strong cyclists can take on the epic sweeping descents of Honister Pass or Newlands Hause (expert level). A gentler approach is via Lorton and Crummock Water.

There is very limited car parking in Buttermere; there is a small Lake District National Park car park (parking charge) and toilets in Buttermere village (next to The Fish Inn) or the National Trust car park (parking charge), which is a short walk from Buttermere village in the direction of Crummock Water. Limited free parking can be found above Buttermere village beyond the church. At the head of the lake there is a small car park at Gatesgarth Farm (parking charge).

Refreshments

» **Croft House Farm Cafe**, Buttermere village. This cafe has wooden benches for seating, positioned over long, low radiators. What could be better after a chilly swim than a warm bum and close proximity to cake!

» **Syke Farm Tearoom**, Buttermere village. Serves amazing home-made ice cream and delicious cakes, and now dog friendly inside. This is my top recommendation for those with dietary requirements, offering an unrivalled selection of gluten-free, dairy-free and vegan food.

» There are also two great pubs in Buttermere village – **The Fish Inn** and **The Bridge Hotel**, both serving hearty fare for hungry swimmers.

General notes on Buttermere

From 1 April until 30 June the National Trust close a section of the northern shore to protect nesting sandpipers. Gates are locked to prevent access; swimmers on an end-to-end or point-to-point swim should be aware for exiting the lake. *www.nationaltrust.org.uk/buttermere-valley/features/spring-wildlife-in-buttermere-valley*

Although boats are allowed by permit you will rarely see one. Buttermere is peaceful on, in and around the water. A permit is also required to launch a canoe, kayak or paddleboard.

Opposite Your author delighted with late March snow on High Crag

CRUMMOCK WATER

Opposite Low Fell above Crummock Water   **Overleaf** The view from Lanthwaite Wood

Lanthwaite Wood & the boathouse

Low Ling Crag

Hause Point

Woodhouse Islands

Introduction

'Crummock Water? Is that on the way to Buttermere?'

Often described as a lesser-known gem of the Western Lakes, Crummock Water is definitely quieter than its more popular neighbour, Buttermere. It has no village or town on its shores and there are just a handful of dwellings. It is a place I frequently see drivers quickly pulling over to take photos; a quick stop on the Lakes tour before the main prize. And what a gem people are passing by.

Crummock Water is twice as long as Buttermere and shares its dramatic scenery. The two lakes were once joined and now an alluvial plain separates them. It creates an optical illusion from the water where Buttermere dips out of view and the mountainous scenery at the head of Buttermere becomes absorbed into the landscape of Crummock Water.

Its relative wilderness is part of the attraction for me. On high days and holidays Crummock Water will be much quieter as ice cream day-trippers stream into Buttermere.

Surrounded by some of my favourite hills, I feel quite at home out in the middle of Crummock Water. I love the unique perspective it gives on a familiar mountain landscape. These hills – Grasmoor, Whiteless Pike, Whiteside and its majestic ridge to Hopegill Head, and of course darling Mellbreak – were my playground before I took time out to care for my dad during his illness. During that period I didn't have time to climb them, but I could swim out to gaze up at the summits; the kick of cold water was as good as topping out on Grasmoor after a long climb through Gasgale Gill.

A big tick for Crummock Water is the sheer ease of access. There are several rudimentary car parks along the eastern shore, all free to use, and you can be in the water within minutes. On the western shore the entire lake is there for the taking, simply by breaking trail wherever you feel like it. In some respects this was a tough list to compile as so much of the shoreline is easily accessible.

Some lakes boast a superlative or diminutive statistic to impress you, others have boat rides and visitor attractions. Or maybe Wordsworth was inspired to write a poem about them. Crummock Water doesn't have a hook to lure you in. It doesn't need one. Take my word for it – Crummock Water is a stone-cold classic.

Opposite Rannerdale Knotts, Red Pike and Mellbreak

Low Ling Crag

I'm not given to having definitive favourites but I'll make an exception for Low Ling Crag. The walk starts with a bucolic wander down a lane through Highpark passing the monolith face of Mellbreak which wouldn't look out of place in an alpine landscape. The path climbs through Green Wood and pops out above Crummock Water to a sublime view down the lake to Rannerdale and the Buttermere fells beyond. Continue along the lakeshore path to the obvious promontory of Low Ling Crag.

Low Ling Crag is a rare Lake District example of a tombolo. Over time, sediment has built up between a rocky mound in the lake and the land forming two perfect crescent beaches on opposite sides. The smooth shingle found here makes it a joy to walk into the water barefoot. It's a place I escape to on busy summer days.

This swim and walk is not complete without a pint of Loweswater Gold, best drunk in the beer garden of The Kirkstile Inn gazing up at Mellbreak.

Lanthwaite Wood & the boathouse

The beach at Lanthwaite Wood is a place to really appreciate the water clarity as it washes over the rocky shingle that lines the shore. It's the first glimpse of Crummock Water as you walk from the National Trust car park, making the beach very popular with visitors and locals alike. It stays relatively shallow here with no shelves to watch out for, ideal for paddling, however you should avoid swimming or paddling too close to the strong tugging current feeding into the weir and fish ladders. Signs around this area indicate United Utilities ownership – swimming around the weir is prohibited.

The beach is quite public. If it is busy, I walk the extra five minutes to the boathouse which also benefits from the shore being gentler underfoot. Sometimes I swim to the line of Scots pines on the opposite shore but mostly I like to swim just far enough to gaze up at the unique view of Grasmoor as it looms above Lanthwaite Wood.

On a windy day it's often calmer close to shore here, protected by the small wooded headland at this narrow neck of the lake.

1 Whiteless Pike viewed from Low Ling Crag   2 Be safe be seen: Lanthwaite boathouse
3 Red Pike and Ling Comb from Low Ling Crag   4 Crummock Water
5 A thing of beauty, and Ali   6 Lifeguard Rosie at Lanthwaite Wood

Hause Point

Before the modern B5289 road existed travellers used a packhorse route that crossed a low shoulder on Rannerdale Knotts. A path remains so you can continue to follow this old way; it is the perfect vantage point over Crummock Water. With the advent of motorised charabancs which ferried tourists along scenic routes, rock was blasted to build a road hugging the hillside instead of going over it. This created an exposed edifice which has long attracted local teenagers who compete to make the most elaborate leap into the water. If, like me, you'd rather not teeter on the narrow ledge, you're in luck. A small beach is tucked away below the road, perfect for a more civilised entry into the water. Don't be alarmed if you see bubbles appearing beside you. It's just a warning sign that a member of the West Cumbria diving club is due to surface nearby (and they will be just as surprised to see you!).

Hause Point and Low Ling Crag mark the narrowest part of Crummock Water. A width of the lake here crosses the deepest part of the lake. As you swim out from Rannerdale, about halfway across the lake, and start to approach Low Ling Crag you may become aware of a slight current. It is quite minor but on occasion I've had to swim a little harder to stay on course as I approach the opposite shore.

Woodhouse Islands

This is one of my regular pull-up-and-swim places – it offers a near perfect opportunity to jump out of the car and straight into the water. I swim here all year round. In winter we shiver on the shore contemplating a fast and furious thrash to the island and back again. In summer we enjoy lazy laps of the islands being careful not to graze knees on the just submerged rocks.

Extend the swim and adventure out to Holme Islands and Scale Island to complete the island trilogy. Lots of birds nest on these islands, beautiful oystercatchers, bean geese, Canada geese and goosanders. I steer clear during nesting season when geese will sail past like angry, feathered galleon ships, giving you a haughty honk if you stray too close.

1 Grasmoor above Lanthwaite Wood **2** Underwater wildlife © Suzanna Cruickshank **3** Woodhouse Islands © Stuart Holmes **4** Crummock Water **5** Whiteless Pike and Rannerdale Knotts from Low Ling Crag **6** Crummock Water

Technical information

MAXIMUM DEPTH **43.9 metres**   AVERAGE DEPTH **26.7 metres**   LENGTH **2.53 miles**   MAXIMUM WIDTH **0.53 miles**
PRIMARY INFLOWS **Buttermere Dubs, Scale Beck, Mill Beck**   OUTFLOW **River Cocker**

Getting there

As with Buttermere, I recommend leaving your car behind and taking the Honister Rambler (77/77A), Easter to October only, which runs along the eastern shore of Crummock Water. All the swimming locations apart from Low Ling Crag are within walking distance and the driver will let you off at an unscheduled stop if the road is clear.

Cyclists can approach from Lorton or over Whinlatter Pass (a challenging option) or from Buttermere.

Parking is available at the National Trust car park at Lanthwaite Wood (parking charge) which is north of Crummock Water, and at Lanthwaite Green, Cinderdale Common and Rannerdale on the eastern shore. There is limited roadside parking near Woodhouse Islands.

Refreshments

» **New House Farm Tea Room**, Lorton. This is often closed for weddings but if they're open, make time to call in and take afternoon tea in the cattle byres.
» **Lorton Village Shop** is an asset to the local area. You can buy most basics here with a strong local and environmentally friendly flavour. Coffee and cake are also available, and you can pick up a locally made souvenir. Stock up for a picnic!

For other nearby options see the suggestions for Buttermere and Loweswater (see pages 138 and 160).

Opposite Lanthwaite Wood

LOWES-WATER

Opposite Burnbank Fell across Loweswater   **Overleaf** Last light on Grasmoor

Waterend
To Ullock
Hudson Place
Darling Fell
Low Fell
N
0   500m
To B5289 &
Cockermouth

Loweswater

Roadside

Holme Beck
Holme Force

Holme Wood

Crabtree Beck
Foulsyke
Highcross
Godferhead
River Cocker
Dub Beck

Watergate Farm

Loweswater

Kirkhead
Park Beck
Crummock Water

Lowpark

Introduction

Of all the lakes, I have never actually seen anyone else swimming in Loweswater. I don't often see more than a handful of people walking around Loweswater either. It's the place to go for a reliably quiet experience. The pastoral lake and village are tucked away in the north-western corner of the Lake District in a much quieter, less dramatic landscape. The lower slopes of Burnbank Fell are densely wooded right down to the lakeshore. In spring, the slumberous woodland is carpeted with bluebells. On the northern shore overhanging trees line the road giving you only tantalising glimpses of water as you pass by. Life is oh so peaceful here, private and intimate.

Loweswater nearly didn't feature in this guidebook. Not only did I struggle to find anyone willing to say that it is swimmable, the lake regularly suffered from blue-green algae blooms. Algae flourished during the warmer months, turning a lurid green at the height of summer, rendering the water unsuitable for swimming. I canvassed opinion from local residents, fell runners and fellow swimmers with responses ranging from 'Och no, it's fine' to 'Eww. No thanks'.

Still unsure, Ali and I walked through the woods to Holme Wood Bothy on a crisp spring day. We hopped on the rope swings and gazed across to a snow-clad Grasmoor. The view, coupled with the calm water, was irresistible. We came back at the first opportunity, cap and goggles in hand. Just through the gate into the wood we set our bags down in the lee of the wall and waded in. After establishing that no, it was not as cold as we thought it would be (it never is), we struck out for the bothy swimming parallel to the shore.

The subject of blue-green algae has been much discussed and is often misunderstood. It's important to note that algae can and does appear in many lakes and it is not always the toxic variety. Historically, algae blooms were more prevalent due to Loweswater's small size and unique ecological situation. In previous years you could reliably find swathes of algae blooms around the edges of the lake. Now, thanks to hard work by members of the Loweswater Care Programme, the National Trust and local farmers, Loweswater is an ever-improving picture. On my most recent visit after a long dry spell, the perfect conditions for algae growth, there was very little sign of blooms in the water. Come on in, the water is lovely!

Opposite Last light from Holme Wood Bothy

Roadside

At either end of the lake is private land, but the northern shore is accessible. A minor road runs along the northern shore; there are a few lay-bys to park in close to Waterend necessitating a short walk along the quiet, narrow road to get to the water. A path from the road soon dips down to follow the shore and then it's just a case of picking your spot in the stony bays between overhanging boughs. You are more likely to encounter stagnant water on this side of the lake, particularly through the summer, as very little fresh water enters the lake due to the lack of becks and streams running off the fells. In autumn, the view across the lake is a perfect Lakeland scene: golden woodland beneath twin fell tops that catch the morning sun.

Holme Wood

Holme Wood cloaks the lower slopes of Blake Fell and Burnbank Fell. Beautiful in all seasons, it really comes to life in autumn when the Loweswater Pheasant appears. The wood was planted in a pattern of deciduous trees and evergreens to reveal the point of a beak, an eye patch and a wing. The best views are from the track to Watergate Farm or from the slopes of Darling Fell where you can also take in the view towards the Cumbrian coastal plain.

Park at Maggie's Bridge and walk along the farm track towards Watergate Farm and the lake (950 metres). Pass through the gate into Holme Wood and a swimming spot with a small beach appears straight away where you can leave bags and get straight in. Wade over the gravel lake bed which gains depth slowly, leaving no chance of an unwitting plunge. A small stream trickles in from higher up in the wood, keeping this particular corner fresh.

Follow the path further into the wood to the gravel beach in front of Holme Wood Bothy. You can hire the bothy from the National Trust to stay overnight – perfect for an early morning constitutional! Another small beck, originating from higher up in the wood, flows in by the beach, keeping the lake topped up and the temperature cool. The water is deep here and always chilly so non-swimmers and paddlers should be wary.

Continuing along the path there is a gravel peninsula where Holme Beck flows into the lake. The beck originates from higher up the fell. It is worth a diversion to walk deep into the wood to see Holme Force, a beautiful waterfall that splits into two long falls and many pools. Back at the beach, pop your clothes on the bench and plunge in – the constant flow of fresh water provides great conditions for cooling off on a hot day.

1 Holme Wood   2 Loweswater   3 Burnbank Fell from the roadside shore
4 Walking to Loweswater   5 Blake Fell and the Loweswater Pheasant

159

Technical information

MAXIMUM DEPTH **16 metres**   AVERAGE DEPTH **8.4 metres**   LENGTH **1.04 miles**   MAXIMUM WIDTH **0.34 miles**
PRIMARY INFLOWS **Dub Beck, Holme Beck**   OUTFLOW **Dub Beck**

Getting there

There is no public transport going directly to Loweswater; the Honister Rambler (77/77A), Easter to October only, stops at Brackenthwaite which is a two-mile walk from Loweswater, mostly on the road. Loweswater is on National Route 71 of the National Cycle Network.

There is a small, free car park for a handful of carefully parked cars at Maggie's Bridge, at the eastern end of Loweswater. Cross the cattle grid and walk along the track through the meadows towards Watergate Farm to get to the water.

The wonderfully named road Fangs Brow is high above the lake and has magnificent views on the approach. Park up here and combine a circular walk on the old coffin route with a swim.

There is further parking in a few small lay-bys near Waterend at the western end of Loweswater; it's a short walk along the road to the wooded lakeshore path.

Refreshments

There are no facilities at the lake itself.

» **The Kirkstile Inn**, Loweswater. This traditional inn is just half a mile from the lake; a visit is not just recommended, it is practically obligatory.

» **The Grange Country House**, Loweswater. Evening meals are served, bookable in advance. Situated a short walk from Waterend.

General Notes on Loweswater

Rowing boats can be hired from Watergate Farm; permits are required to launch your own boats. Holme Wood Bothy can be booked via the National Trust.
www.nationaltrust.org.uk/holidays/bothy-holme-wood-the-lake-district

Opposite A glimpse of the Loweswater Pheasant in Holme Wood

Reservoirs

With such frequent and unfettered access to open water it is perhaps easier to tell you where you can't swim in the Lake District rather than where you can. In England it's legal to access open water providing you don't have to trespass in order to reach it. There are a few exceptions.

Ennerdale Water, Haweswater and Thirlmere are the three main and best-known reservoirs in the Lake District. They are all situated at valley level and ostensibly give no clues to their true purpose until you look a bit closer. United Utilities own these bodies of water and operate a no swimming policy across all their waters. When it comes to reservoirs, I begrudgingly obey the rules.

I don't believe that a reservoir is more dangerous than a natural lake. But that doesn't mean you should go and swim in one. The ban undoubtedly stems from the private ownership of the water and fear of litigation. In my view an accident in a lake is the same as an accident on a mountain; it's likely to be the fault of the person through misadventure or lack of experience.

Practical information about genuine hazards is scarce. The argument that reservoirs are unsafe because they are deep and cold is misleading. Wast Water, Ullswater and Windermere are all deeper than Thirlmere and Haweswater.

Accidents happen in all waters. Anecdotal evidence suggests that accidents happen in reservoirs because people may unwittingly believe that reservoirs are somehow less wild than a natural lake. People who live a predominantly urban lifestyle may find themselves drawn to the neat information boards, waymarked trails and car parks instead of the wilderness of a mountain valley.

The presence of underwater machinery and strong currents is another reason often given not to swim in reservoirs. There is some truth in both these reasons. It's scientifically plausible that the effects of water being drawn off can create a current similar to an undertow you may experience in the sea. 'Infrastructure' is probably a more accurate description of what you might find under the water than actual moving machinery. Water is drawn off through large diameter pipes and grates or strainers will be present. I have not been able to uncover any reports of accidents in reservoirs directly relating to either machinery or currents.

When researching the no swimming policy the information was predictably vague and responses were cagey. The ruling covering Ennerdale Water is perhaps the most difficult to accept. Not only is it a natural lake (Haweswater and Thirlmere have both been dammed to raise their levels) but it is the only lake with no road alongside it – a peaceful gem we have to admire from afar.

Esthwaite Water is not a reservoir but it's still out of bounds. It's a privately owned fishery in South Cumbria situated between Coniston Water and Windermere. Historically, people did swim in the lake (and still do) and at one time there was an area on the lake named The Swimming Pool. The fishery owners do not permit swimming, partly to protect their liability, although I know people do swim there. Based on water quality reports from those swimmers I am inclined to leave well alone.

Opposite Gillie and Tiger © James Kirby

Further reading

I've sought inspiration and information from various sources while researching this guidebook, some pertaining directly to the Lake District, others purely watery. As you might expect, the internet is a mine of information, both valuable and complete nonsense. Whether you are looking for someone to swim with or some general information, social media is a good place to start. The Outdoor Swimming Society has a very active and friendly Facebook group with geographical offshoots across the country.

Ordnance Survey Explorer 1:25,000 maps
(OL4, OL5, OL6 and OL7)
Ordnance Survey Landranger 1:50,000 maps
(89, 90 and 96)
The humble OS map has always been my first port of call. A 1:25,000 map shows the fine detail while the 1:50,000 indicates depth contours for the lakes.

An Atlas of the English Lakes: Pictorial Charts Compiled from an Exploration of the Shorelines of the Lake District on Foot and by Canoe
John Wilson Parker
Cicerone Press, 2002
A joy to behold. This is a painstakingly researched guide to the Lakes written by a retired Ordnance Survey cartographical surveyor. It's out of print but copies remain in circulation so you can find one if you are lucky. Every swimmer should have one.

The Lake District: The Ultimate Guide
Gordon Readyhough
Hayloft Publishing, 2004
'Ultimate guides' usually make me bristle with an anxious tic. But this compendium of all things Lake District and Cumbria is part list, part encyclopaedia. It's a fascinating reference book. Handy for pub quizzers!

Lakeland: Walking with Wildlife
Alan Gane
Austin Macauley Publishers, 2016
I'm a bit rubbish when it comes to identifying plants and flowers or sparrow-sized birds. There aren't many images in the book but there doesn't need to be as the lovely storytelling takes you on a walk through the rich flora and fauna of the Cumbrian fells.

Rock Trails Lakeland: A Hillwalker's Guide to the Geology and Scenery
Paul Gannon
Pesda Press, 2009
Perfect for a greater understanding of how the hills and lakes were formed with the added bonus of walking routes to see the best examples.

Wild Swim
Kate Rew
Guardian Books, 2008
This beautiful book is a bible for outdoor swimmers. It covers lakes, rivers, seas and lidos across the UK.

The following three books are handy for learning more about the geology and ecology of the Lake District.

Granite and Grit: A Walker's Guide to the Geology of British Mountains
Ronald Turnbull
Frances Lincoln, 2011

Lake District Mountain Landforms
Peter Wilson
Scotforth Books, 2010

The Geology of the Lake District
Robert Westwood
Inspiring Places Publishing, 2009

How to Read Water: Clues, Signs & Patterns from Puddles to the Sea
Tristan Gooley
Sceptre, 2016
An eminently handy guide to all things wet, this useful guide offers explanations to why water behaves the way it does.

Swimhiking in the Lake District and North East England
Peter Hayes
Gilbert Knowle Publishers, 2008
An eccentric and entertaining tale of swimhiking across the Lake District, packed with seagull conspiracies. The birthplace of the 'Frog Graham' – a swimmer's take on the legendary Bob Graham twenty-four-hour fell running challenge.

Open Water Swimming Manual: An Expert's Survival Guide for Triathletes and Open Water Swimmers
Lynne Cox
Penguin Random House, 2013
There are a plethora of books on swimming technique available; this one is written with a passion and joy that underpins the technical side. I swim for enjoyment over exercise but appreciate that efficient movement in the water will improve any experience. This is the only book on swimming technique that I have ever finished. And kept.

Outdoor Swimmer
www.outdoorswimmer.com
A monthly dose of the UK outdoor swimming scene distilled into paper (or digital) form. A perfect balance of swimming wild and free, with international news, extraordinary swimming feats, and articles to inspire.

UK Lakes Portal
https://eip.ceh.ac.uk/apps/lakes
Database of bodies of water in the UK containing a copious amount of interesting information.

Acknowledgements

Although the words and research are all my own, the energy and enthusiasm behind this project has been the combined efforts of a small group of friends. The guidebook wouldn't have happened had it not been for the unfailing moral and practical support of Ali Mosedale, Anna Jacobs, Ella Foote, Fiona Williams, Lottie Thompson, Ian Wade and Tim Mosedale, all of whom gave their time freely and without question. I would also like to thank Stuart Holmes for his valuable wisdom and guidance on the finer points of publishing a guidebook.

Thank you to Jude Gale for encouraging me to swim further than I thought I could. For teaching me to swim front crawl and coaching my technique for all situations. For cooking substantial meals of dubious origin. But above all, thank you for being an inspiring, positive influence and giving me focus during a difficult stage in my life.

Stewart Smith photographed most of the images in this book and I am eternally grateful for his work on the project. He fitted the shoots around his regular photography work and we met at ungodly and awkward hours to capture the best light and conditions. My photography brief was vague to say the least, but with Stewart's help the project went from pipe dream to viable reality.

I have contributed some of my own images and would like to thank Alicja Zazusha for the generous and unlimited loan of her GoPro camera, which now lies at the bottom of Bassenthwaite Lake. I'd also like to thank Dr Jonathan Nicholson for the generous and unlimited loan of his GoPro camera which sadly met its demise in Wast Water. I'm hoping the third incarnation will survive a little longer.

Additional images contributed by Andrew Locking, Anita Nicholson, Carmen Norman, James Kirby and Stuart Holmes.

I entrusted copies of the first draft of this guidebook to Diana Clarke, Ella Foote, Jackie Risman and Tim Mosedale, who gave their honest and insightful opinions, as did fellow author Alex Roddie.

Thank you to Colin Hill for a wonderful boat ride across Ullswater and for imparting some real gems of information about the lake. Colin knows Ullswater better than anyone and guides exclusively from Another Place Hotel on Ullswater.

Thank you to Pete and Andrea Kelly for their kind support and advice. Their shop in Ambleside, Swim the Lakes, is the place to go for all your outdoor swimming equipment needs as well as guided group swims and private coaching.

Some of the photos required a view from a boat. Thanks to Andrew Graham and Samuel Graham for Derwent Water, Anna Jacobs for Coniston Water and Geoff Williams for Ullswater. And to Stewart Smith for not complaining one bit about the precarious situations I put him in.

Thank you to William Carruthers of Bassenthwaite Sailing Club, Jonathon at High Bank Ground and Roger Hiley for patiently answering questions and sharing information about their local areas.

A book filled with photos of me swimming around the Lake District would be vastly unrepresentative. I'd like to thank all my swim models for taking part and sharing their favourite places with me:

Ailie Tonkin, Aleks Kashefi, Ali Mosedale, Amy Fazzalaro, Colin Hill, Emma McKnespiey, Fiona Williams, Francine Wells, Grace Mosedale, Ian Wade, Jenny Rice, Jude Gale, Lorna Singleton, Lottie Thompson, Max Mosedale, Paul Dobson, Paul Scully, Pete Kelly, Susan Cartwright-Smith, Tim Mosedale and, finally, director of Jogging Pals and all round nice guy, Wayne Singleton.

Thank you!

LAKE DISTRICT
GUIDEBOOKS & NARRATIVES

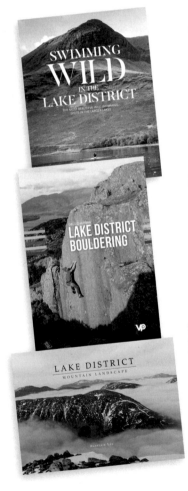

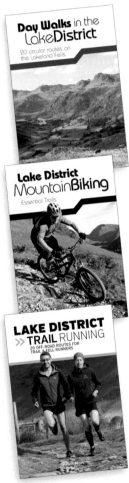

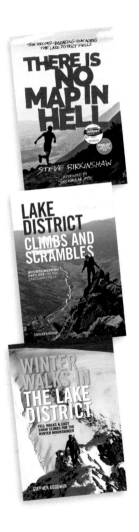

vp inspiring adventure

Available from book shops or direct from
www.v-publishing.co.uk